Our Natural Potential

Beyond Personal Development
The Stages of Enlightenment

Our Natural Potential

Beyond Personal Development
The Stages of Enlightenment

David "Davidya" Buckland

Davidya Publishing

Our Natural Potential
Beyond Personal Development
The Stages of Enlightenment

David "Davidya" Buckland, MA

Published by Davidya Publishing
Courtenay, BC, Canada V9N 3W5
books@davidya.ca
www.davidya.ca/books/

Library and Archives Canada Cataloguing in Publication

Buckland, David, 1954-, author
    Our natural potential : beyond personal development : the stages of enlightenment / David "Davidya" Buckland.

Includes bibliographical references and index.
Issued in print and electronic formats.
ISBN 978-0-9959837-0-0 (softcover).--ISBN 978-0-9959837-1-7 (Kindle).--ISBN 978-0-9959837-2-4 (EPUB).--ISBN 978-0-9959837-3-1 (PDF)

    1. Consciousness. 2. Transpersonal psychology. 3. Maturation (Psychology). 4. Self-actualization (Psychology). I. Title.

BF311.B83 2017   153   C2017-903190-2
                                                          C2017-903191-0

Dedication

This book is dedicated to my parents. Their support allowed life, insight, and work to unfold in ways that none of us anticipated.

Deepest Gratitude To

Bharadvaja Barhaspatya
Swami Brahamanda Saraswati
Maharishi Mahesh Yogi
Lorne & Lucia Hoff

They have been key spiritual influences
in recent lives.

Table of Contents

Tables and Lists

Foreword

The Inuits have 50 words for snow. Fiji islanders have none. Eastern spiritual traditions have hundreds of terms for various higher states and stages of consciousness. The predominant scientific Western paradigm has but a few. Eastern spiritual traditions regard consciousness as the foundation and ultimate constituent of creation. The materialist paradigm dismisses consciousness as merely an epiphenomenon of brain functioning and insists that when the body dies, we cease to exist.

The West has seen an influx of Eastern spirituality over the past hundred years, and particularly since the 60s, but hasn't possessed the experiential basis nor the conceptual framework to integrate this knowledge readily. The Buddhist and Vedic traditions possess such a framework, but contemporary representatives actually experiencing higher states, and thus able to grasp the full range and subtlety of their own traditions, have been rare. When they have existed, they have usually been unfamiliar with Western culture. Communicating with it has involved a learning curve.

Most of the teachers who came west attempted to integrate their teachings with science, contending that their methods were amenable to scientific experimentation. Some – most notably Maharishi Mahesh Yogi and the

Dalai Lama – actively worked with scientists to conduct research on their students. They hoped that higher states of consciousness might be understood objectively and thus become demystified and more readily accepted in the West. To date, hundreds of studies on Transcendental Meditation, vipassana, mindfulness, Zen, and other practices have been conducted.

The practitioners of these disciplines have been researchers of a different sort. Their scientific "instrument" has been their own mind and nervous system, the realm of their investigation their own consciousness. Many have been conducting this research for decades, and quite a few of them have replicated what their ancient Eastern counterparts discovered - that we each can access a "Heaven within." We possess the ability to radically transform our experience of ourselves and the world and to live life as wise, blissful "knowers of reality."

Such people are becoming more commonplace. I've interviewed hundreds of them on my show *Buddha at the Gas Pump*[1] and have a never-ending queue of others yet to interview. One thing this has taught me is that as the perennial wisdom of enlightenment has taken root and proliferated in the West, its growth has been rather unruly. There is no universal understanding of what enlightenment is, what the stages of its development are, or how one who has attained it might be expected to behave or function in the world.

Consequently, there is some consistency but much divergence among spiritual teachers and their teachings. They and their students (and others who reject the necessity of teachers altogether) often mistake intellectual understanding for experiential realization, preliminary spiritual awakenings for final ones (thus losing the incentive to continue), and/or vary widely on the importance of techniques and practices and ethical guidelines.

I feel that a few generations from now, people will look back on our era as the beginning of a profound societal transformation. The attainment of higher states of consciousness by a significant percentage of the population will be seen to have been the ultimate source of the solutions to problems which came close to extinguishing most life on earth, including human. Science and spirituality - objective and subjective means of gaining knowledge - will have become two aspects of a unified endeavor.

But for this prediction to be realized, it won't be enough for people to engage in spiritual practices or for scientists to study them. Those who genuinely attain higher states of consciousness will have to contribute to the development of a clear, systematic, nuanced, and consensual understanding of these states.

Getting back to our snow metaphor, I consider David Buckland an Inuit of consciousness. His decades of deeply fruitful spiritual practice, coupled with his extensive intellectual study of the Vedic and other traditions, plus his many interactions with people experiencing various stages of awakening have afforded him an intellectual and experiential "filing cabinet" in which any spiritual utterance easily finds its rightful place.

Many spiritual aspirants assume or are taught that there is one watershed breakthrough which can universally be agreed upon as final "Realization." They are discouraged from thinking that there might be many degrees and stages of realization, each of them important stepping-stones in a never-ending journey. They are told that if we regard spiritual development as progressive, we will forever be anticipating, never arriving. I've even interviewed people who have said, "If you like your life, don't seek enlightenment. You may not like it and you'll be stuck with it."

In this book, David effectively dispels that notion. What some might regard as a final destination, he regards as a good foundation upon which to build much more profound, gratifying stages of development. Some might regard his presentation as overly complicated and prefer simple expressions such as "there is just this," but that's comparable to someone with a rudimentary appreciation of music saying that Beethoven's 5th symphony "sounds good" vs. a maestro who can discern and explain fine details in and between performances.

I've been reading David's blog[2] for years. I always learn something. I have a feeling this won't be David's last book. In it, he alludes to some fascinating topics that I hope he'll elaborate on in future books. But this one presents an inspiring vision of possibilities. You'll probably want to re-read it periodically as these possibilities become actualities in your own life.

Rick Archer
Buddha at the Gas Pump
July 16, 2017

Notes
1 batgap.com
2 davidya.org

Preface

This book takes a philosophical and academic approach to model and understand our higher potential. But it is built on direct experience rather than concepts.

This includes both historical descriptions and the experience of myself and many others. I also formally studied Vedic science and world religions in graduate school.

There's some irony in using my personal experience as a credential for writing about post-personal development. Yet it is valuable for the reader to understand where I'm coming from as it certainly informs the content.

To avoid being redundant, I refer to the sequence of events here but more details of each shift are described in the Examples section of each stage. This will give them more context.

In my late teens, I began reading about consciousness and brain organization, then started Transcendental Meditation (TM) in 1974. I quickly became an avid spiritual explorer, attending many talks and courses. Within the year, I arrived in northeastern France for a six-month retreat to deepen my understanding and train to become a teacher of TM.

After 3 months of extra meditations, asana, and pranayama with lots of purification and clearing, I had sporadic witnessing experiences where awareness shifted briefly into a detached observer mode. Then in the second 3 months, the lights came on within. Thereafter, the observing witness was continuous, throughout waking, dreaming, and sleeping. That has never ended although it has certainly deepened.

Soon after that, the first cognition happened. A cognition is a type of experience where everything about the object is known: all values of perception, its structure, history, the works. (This is the "basic" type I discuss later in the book.)

Here, it was hiranya gharba or the golden egg, the seed and origin of our universe. Essentially, this was experiencing the entire universe from the outside as well as the mechanics of its manifestation.

It took months for the mind to unpack this experience. At the end of the course, Maharishi Mahesh Yogi confirmed the experiences and said there would be much more.

As I returned to normal life, it became clear that Self was awake but ego remained identified. Self had not yet woken up to itself. I explore variations like this in the book.

Subtle perception continued to unfold. I soon began experiencing divine beings but because of prior experience with more base attention-seeking entities I was circumspect with them for a while. I wanted to be sure this wasn't just misleading appearances.

However, the divine beings did point out things that allowed me to unfold awareness of the structure of creation prior to our universe. For example, Krishna pointed out a feature of the "sky" above the golden egg that led awareness beyond this space into the larger space of creation.

This combination of experiences led to some deep questioning. I was experiencing the primary symptoms of the first two stages of enlightenment. Yet it was clear they were just experiences. I was also being shown the structure of reality in a more advanced way than anything I'd heard of. Yet if I shared any of it, there was significant negative feedback from people in positions of authority. It became clear that it was better to keep it within and let things mature.

Gradually, spiritual development shifted to the back burner while work, then marriage and children came to dominate. Practical life helped ground and integrate what was developing and cultured the physiology further.

In 2005, the life I had been living wound down and the spiritual side unexpectedly moved back to the forefront.

I reconnected with some old friends and a few it turned out had become self-realized. After some feedback and darshan with Lorne Hoff, Self at last woke up to Itself during a conference call in July, 2007.

I then began attending retreats with Lorne and Lucia. This helped the growth but also brought experiences of seeing many others awaken. When it's the same Self waking nearby, it is something of a shared experience. As people progressed, there were many examples of higher stages as well.

The God Consciousness stage arrived about 2 months after the first shift with a profound heart opening and overflowing.

About 2 months after that, another process began. There was the brief roasting of the final "core identity" in the gut and the end of the sense of "David." Soon after on a retreat, all the prior awakening and experiences fell away, and there was a shift into Unity.

As Unity develops, it progressively moves into all layers of experience. At a certain point, the oneness moved right into the senses. Touching an object, I felt it. But as I was also the object, I felt being touched simultaneously. These sorts of experiences created a deep intimacy with all of life.

Then Refined Unity unfolded, including a deeper relationship with the divine and the personal God. The devata and cosmic bodies became known as well as the "body of God." As I became the cosmic body, a process of the body itself waking up began.

By the fall of 2010, I was in grad school studying Vedic science. It was a compressed program with classes 6 days a week that required my undivided attention. I had become aware of consciousness globally, as well as at every point. But most attention was on studies.

During a meditation in a large dome with many others, another surrender began. There was then a shift and "everything everywhere" was absorbed by a transparent nothing. Consciousness was transcended into an unmanifest source. The relationship with the personal God ended along with the former intimacy with the world.

At the time, it was not my understanding that consciousness was transcended in the Brahman shift so this came as a surprise and took more time to process. It also began an unusual dry period. I expected this to end quickly but it didn't. However, there was little time to digest what had transpired.

By the time I finished grad school, there was a deeper embodiment of the shift and I had more time to process the changes. The following year, there was a still deeper heart opening and sense of divinity.

Finally, divinity returned in the new context, then pure Divinity began to be recognized and embodied. The process continues.

If it's of interest, I described this process in a Buddha at the Gas Pump interview[1] in 2015.

As you'll see, this book is not a list of hollow concepts but a living process I'm observing unfold in and around me. A new era in human potential is dawning and a framework to support that unfolding is needed. That is why I compiled this book.

Notes
1 batgap.com/david-davidya-buckland

Introduction

Know Thyself
— Greek aphorism[1]

This is a work of love that began years ago when I started a long exploration of our natural potential. In the 1970's, there was a wave of new books on the brain, mind, and consciousness. Then Maharishi Mahesh Yogi's model of seven states of consciousness was published by author Tom Campbell. Books like the *Tao of Physics* were also produced. But more importantly, many millions of people around the world took up meditation, including myself. Philip Goldberg's book *American Veda* summarizes the time and people well. Fast forward a few decades and some of those people "woke up" to their deeper, unlimited nature beyond their individuality. This shift is known as spiritual awakening or enlightenment.

Maharishi stopped referring to those states by the

mid-1980's and focused on Brahman, a later post-consciousness stage. When my own unfolding flowered, I was fortunate to also witness the shifts in many others.

In 2010, I headed to graduate school to study Vedic Science and its ancient understanding of this process. This gave me a broader view that led to a new synthesis. I distinguished the stages of development in consciousness from the related refinement process, separated states of the physiology from stages of development, and added post-consciousness stages. This better reflected the unfolding I was observing in and around me.

This book will explore the result of this synthesis in some detail. It offers a model for understanding the unfolding of post-personal development or enlightenment.

But first, let's review some background to help understand the nature of this development.

Consciousness

As post-personal development is primarily about consciousness, let's examine how we know it. We can say the following.

Consciousness is Experienced Four Ways.

1) states of consciousness we cycle through daily: waking, dreaming, and sleeping. These are more accurately described as states of the physiology that affect our awareness.

2) altered states of consciousness, typically induced by drugs, intense practices, or unusual experiences. These are altered experiences of physiological states, the first type.

3) the state of empty consciousness itself (Transcendental Consciousness or Presence). This is first noticed as a brief state and later comes to be known as the ground of being, always with us.

4) stages of development in consciousness, each of which brings a distinct sense of self and the world. These also reveal the nature of consciousness itself.

Consciousness has a 3-fold Nature.
a) the observer or experiencer, that which is aware[2]
b) the process of observing or experiencing
c) the observed or objects of experience

In Sanskrit, these are known as Rishi, Devata, and Chhandas, respectively.

We can use the analogy of going to a movie theater. There is the audience or watcher, the process of watching, and the movie being watched. With an empty theater, there is no watcher, there is no watching, and no movie being seen – even if the projector is running. Alternately, without the movie there is no movie being watched, even if someone is in the theater. If the movie is playing and the watcher starts daydreaming, then the process is directed within and no movie is being seen either. It takes all three for the experience of the movie.

While this may seem very abstract, the distinctions are

key to understanding the different stages. If researchers and practitioners don't distinguish experiences (the content) from consciousness itself, there can be a tendency to chase experiences and altered states. While experiences can certainly be entertaining, they don't move us along. Induced altered states also have a host of documented hazards and are inherently transitory, distort perception, and can create energetic residues that reduce clarity. This can be a serious impediment to progress in consciousness and quality of life.

Key for stages of development in consciousness is developing awareness of consciousness itself rather than the content.

We'll be exploring this in a framework of 3 stages and the parallel process of refinement.

> *The soul walks not upon a line,*
> *neither does it grow like a reed.*
> *The soul unfolds itself,*
> *like a lotus of countless petals.*
> — Kahlil Gibran, The Prophet

This work is not designed to give simple, black and white explanations. Human development is a diverse, complex, and messy thing. The goal here is to point to the underlying process and note some of the variations in how that is experienced. In that way, you can use it as a general map for your own journey and put the works of many saints and sages into some context. It can also serve as a framework for research.

Models

Some spiritual teachers reject these kinds of concepts as a barrier to living them. This is true; until we know it directly, our concepts will always fail us. Our beliefs can be an impediment to seeing what is here. Just consider how well you understood puberty before it unfolded. Stages of development in consciousness are beyond the mind and thus beyond its ability to imagine. But if we have no map, how are we to negotiate the road? How are we to support others in their own unique unfolding? How are we to put various teachings into some context? How are we to research this? I recommend an overview of the path to point the way while remembering the map is not the road. The model is not the reality. And don't forget – a concept of no stages or a concept of barriers has the same issue as a concept of stages. It's holding on to concepts (identification) that is the issue, not the ideas themselves.

> *There is no greater barrier to enlightenment than a mind that thinks it knows what enlightenment is.*
> — Lorne Hoff[3]

The majority of models I've seen do not cover the full range of stages in consciousness. Many describe steps in the approach to the first stage, are missing the parallel refinement process, or stop part way along. Frequently, they are driven by one person's experience of their own process. I've even seen what amounts to a list of someone's experiences.

There is another type of model that focuses on the energetic changes that unfold with growth of consciousness. I've seen models that measure progress based on chakra purity, balance or alignment. Or the rise and descent of kundalini Shakti. However, these are effects with a high variability I'll discuss further along. They relate to purification and embodiment rather than the shifts themselves.

Another orientation is measuring progress in refined perception, such as perception of progressively finer levels of creation*. However, this puts the weight on experiences and certain styles of experience that are not universal. For example, some experience cosmic levels of creation before waking up and some never do.

(* I use the word "creation" to describe the larger container that is inclusive of multiple universes. This is the field of Atman, the cosmic.)

We might consider refined perception and chakra clarity corroborating indicators, but they are not primary. As it is the underlying shifts in consciousness that mark the primary changes, I use that as the baseline.

Another common issue is the diversity of terminology and understanding around these topics. I invite readers to keep an open mind and use the details to "translate" into their language of choice.

This work emphasizes the results of spiritual practice and the forms of awakening that ensue. Being visual, I use visual language. I touch on other varieties throughout but there is a natural bias to what I know. I consider this a work in progress towards a more complete working framework of the journey.

Human Development

To put this work into a larger, more human context, let's touch on early human development. When we're first born, the brain is in overdrive, creating massive connections as we soak up experiences like a sponge. Our brain is functioning in EEG delta mode, like a waking sleep. Our developmental focus is on the senses and motor activity. We learn to interpret and function in the world, to walk and to talk. Over time, the sensory and motor pathways in the brain are myelinated (insulated) into fast, established pathways.

During the preschool "toddler" years, the focus of development shifts to desires and basic emotions. We sometimes call the onset of this the "terrible twos." The number of brain connections soon peaks at about twice the connections of an adult. Our brain functions largely in EEG theta, leaving us in a dreamy, receptive state.

As we reach school years, the mind becomes the focus of development. The brain shifts more into EEG beta frequencies during waking hours. The connections between the two sides of the brain are reinforced and myelinated. Around age 10, considerable pruning of the many little-used connections we made earlier takes place. We thus lose easy access to many of our early memories but become much more efficient at common activities.

During the teens, the intellect and higher brain (forebrain) more fully engage and we gain the potential to explore more abstract thought. The pruning completes by about age 18. As young adults, prefrontal myelination brings our "executive" functions fully on-line. Experiences continue to shape our brain for the rest of our lives.

> *Your brain is a river, not a rock.*
> — Dr. Fred Travis[4]

These stages (Alexander) from psychology correspond with cognitive[5] (Piaget, below), ego[6] (Loevinger) and moral[7] (Kohlberg) developmental models. We can say these are different ways to explore the stages of *personal* development.

Alexander, Cognitive, and Kosha table.

In this chart, we compare the Alexander stages to Piaget's and the Vedic kosha* model:

Age	Area (Alexander)	Cognitive (Piaget)	Kosha* (Vedic)
0-2	Behaviour and Senses	Sensori-motor	Anna-
2-7	Desires and emotions	Pre-operations	Prana-
7-11	Mind	Concrete Operations	Manon-
11-18	Intellect	Formal Operations	Vijnana-
18-25	Feelings and intuition	Post-Formal Ops	"
25+	Individual ego	[Myness]	"
	Universal	[Amness]	Ananda-

(*Kosha is a Sanskrit term for energy sheath or layer of being. See The Layers section below.)

8

Notice how the leading edge of development dominates at each stage. Also, note how each stage is progressively more subtle and abstract but also more powerful and inclusive. And each stage sets the context for how we see others, the world, and ourselves. While we may have become used to how we see the world now, we've not seen it this way for large periods of our own lives. We sometimes forget that.

Subjectively, the intellect and intuition are two ways of experiencing the same kosha. This is why there aren't two corresponding koshas for those stages. In Samkhya philosophy, ego (ahamkara) is an individuation by the intellect (mahat) and so doesn't have its own kosha.

Many adults stall development in what Loevinger called the Conventional stages of ego development such as "Conformist" and "Self-Aware." This is in the Mind or Concrete Operations stage noted above. Such people have a literal interpretation of the world. But some continue on into post-formal or post-conventional development. First comes the more abstract intellect, then subtle feelings, intuition, and finally, the individual ego itself. Such people become more established as autonomous individuals. This allows what Maslow described as Self-Actualization[8].

(Society at large can develop in similar stages. The dominant level of development of the individuals will dominate the community. We could give such stages names like Survival, Tribal, Individualist, and so forth.)

Maslow later proposed a stage of self-transcendence. Dr. Skip Alexander[9] observed that Eastern models of development of consciousness could be integrated with the Western models of psychology at this juncture. A branch of psychology known as transpersonal was also developed to look at post-personal stages. Dr. Cook-Greuter[10] proposed Construct-Aware and Unitive stages of the ego.

This points to enlightenment or spiritual awakening as part of our natural potential. But in the cycles of time, those habits of life and understanding that culture higher development became lost in the struggle to survive or fit in. These more developed stages then became much more rare. But that is changing now. The opportunity for growth has increased markedly in the last 30 years and even more so in the last decade. We need upgraded models to help support the shifts happening the world over.

> *This is a time of the ordinary awakening. This means you. Not those born under the brightest stars, but the ordinary person as well.*
> — Gangaji[11]

Keep in mind this is an experiential process. It is not about building concepts. Even if you feel you understand consciousness, until it is a lived embodiment, concepts remain a shadow of it. It is also hazardous to use any conceptual scale to judge oneself or another. The point of this is to support your journey, not turn it into a story or critique. Again, don't confuse the map with the road.

The Layers

Dr. Alexander described the layers of development

mentioned above: body, emotions, mind, intellect, feelings, and ego. Then we move into stages of development in consciousness itself, what he described as "post-representation" stages.

The Vedic model for the layers that give rise to these experiences is known as the koshas or sheaths.

The 7 Koshas
Annamaya kosha: the "food" or physical body
Pranamaya kosha: the "breath" or emotional/energy body
Manonmaya kosha: the mind and senses
Vijnanamaya kosha: the intellect and intuition
Anandamaya kosha: the bliss, celestial, or causal body (semi-universal)
Chittamaya kosha: the "flow" or consciousness with direction (universal)
Atmamaya kosha: consciousness, Atman, or Cosmic Self

Note that the name of each kosha includes "maya." This refers to creation, not illusion. I explore this further in the Self Realization section below.

Most teachings mention only the first five koshas. This is the reality through Self Realization. Later the other two layers become known, and it is discovered that Atman (consciousness) is also a layer of being or sheath.

Consciousness is the last, subtlest, and primary layer. Philosophers and scientists are gradually recognizing that consciousness is not an accidental side effect of brain functioning but is fundamental to who we are. Being fundamental, it is universal. David Chalmers[12] and Bernardo Kastrup[13] have discussed the scientifically "Hard Problem of Consciousness" through logic.

11

Verifying that consciousness is a fundamental property of our being becomes much clearer when we have the direct experience of the fourth state of consciousness, described shortly.

The energetic sludge that interferes with clarity of experience and quality of life is stored in the upper three koshas. The fourth level (intellect) can have mistakes of association and energetic crusts but is relatively clear itself.

The Chakras

We have seven primary chakras (energy centers) that run vertically down the spine from the crown to the base of the spine. Chakra means wheel and they function like energy sources to feed the koshas above and run the layers of our physiology. They are not physical. They form the energetic structure to support life (prana or chi).

The chakras exist in a straight line and are equidistant. There is also just one set expressed in the bliss body that is shared by all beings in this universe. When the chakras are expressed into the grosser koshas, they become more specialized. They can then be perceived in various ways – like a geometry, like a flower with petals and roots, like spinning energy, like a sound or feeling, or like a vortex or cone. Different kinds of beings express different values of each. In our body, these expressions move with us and are not perfectly equidistant. They can even be out of alignment.

From the chakras, thousands of major and minor nadis (energy channels) radiate out into the body, forming the energetic substrate for the nervous, circulatory, and lymphatic systems. The nadis are fine subtle tubes, created by the flow of awareness continuously curving back on itself in a gentle spiral.

> *Among all these nadis, 72 thousand are important. Of these, 100 are principal. And of these, three are particularly significant. Of these three, the most important is the sushumna, which extends from the base of the spine to the crown of the head.*
> — Swami Muktananda, *Secret of the Siddhas*

The nadis are also where a lot of the aforementioned energetic debris is stored, much as plaque can build up in our arteries.

The chakras also each have an array of fifty radiating nadis that Rose Rosetree calls "chakra databanks." Rather than traveling out to other nadis and the periphery of the body, they radiate like a spiky Christmas ornament. They carry our gifts and mark the local expression of the cosmic devata (light beings, laws of nature) that "operate" that chakra and structure our form.

Often, the chakras are portrayed as a series of single-coloured discs in a tidy rainbow sequence. However, they are normally each multi-coloured and widely variable over time in each person. They are mainly what generate our aura colours. While the original 7 chakras in the anandamaya kosha are single colours each, I would not describe them as a rainbow nor as colours we see with eyes and have names for.

I've seen models of development suggesting that as we

grow, we identify with a progressively higher chakra. We can see how this would relate to the koshas and stages mentioned in the prior sections. For example, identified with the mind would be supported mainly by the 3rd chakra and kosha. Identified with consciousness or awake would mean the 7th chakra and kosha. But the process in consciousness is somewhat distinct from the rise of kundalini Shakti, discussed further along.

I've seen references to more chakras above the head. Some people describe a rise above the head into higher "dimensions." However, I've only seen Westerners refer to this. I was shown that the higher ones are actually the original seven at higher octaves (koshas). The post-awakening energy descends as a higher octave or resolution of the original chakras. For example, where the heart chakra (4, anahata) woke during the rise, the divine value (10, hridaya) awakens during the descent, usually with the God Consciousness stage (described shortly), to whatever value the nervous system is prepared to experience it. A chart can help illustrate how we might count more than 7 chakras.

The Chakras

7	>	Crown	\/	
6	/\	Third eye	\/	8
5	/\	Throat	\/	9
4	/\	Heart	\/	10
3	/\	Solar Plexus	\/	11
2	/\	Gonads	\/	12
1	/\	Root	<	

See how the 8th is a higher 6th, the 9th a higher 5th and so forth? The crown and root are the ends of the loop and so remain the same. This leads us to a "12 chakra" model. But fundamentally, it remains just 7. I'm sure there are other ways this is experienced but I'd be careful not to add extras based on subjective variety alone.

Energy unfolding is not a tidy linear process. Additionally, there is a difference between how it might be subjectively experienced and the actual process taking place. Is a release in one place triggering emotions or sensations elsewhere? Is a flash in the head due to makara, or is it an effect of the pranas merging in the gut? Whole traditions are often built on the subjective experiences of a few people with a specific practice. Key is to understand that the energy process is not causal but plays a supportive role in helping us to prepare for and embody the shifts.

Notes

1 Various attributions
2 davidya.ca/2014/08/09/awareness-becomes-self-aware
3 Spoken, fall 2007
4 Book title, (2012)
5 en.wikipedia.org/wiki/Piaget%27s_theory_of_cognitive_development
6 en.wikipedia.org/wiki/Loevinger%27s_stages_of_ego_development
7 en.wikipedia.org/wiki/Lawrence_Kohlberg%27s_stages_of_moral_development
8 en.wikipedia.org/wiki/Self-actualization
9 truthabouttm.org/DocumentFiles/26.pdf
10 cook-greuter.com/GatewaytoTransc.2000%202008%20updated.pdf
11 Newsletter 2014-07-21
12 youtu.be/uhRhtFFhNzQ
13 youtu.be/Pp8s_cAl2h4

The Approach

But seek ye first the kingdom of God,
and his righteousness;
and all these things shall be added unto you as well.
— Bible, New Testament, Matthew 6:33[1]

...for the kingdom of God is in your midst (within).
— Bible, New Testament, Luke 17:21

Throughout our early development, most of our experience of "consciousness" is through the 3 states of waking, dreaming, and sleeping. Consciousness does appear to be fleeting and an effect of the state of our body. When tired, our experience is foggy and we want sleep. But there is also a fourth distinct state of consciousness that has been repeatedly demonstrated with scientific research. It is not yet widely recognized though.

This fourth state is known as Restful Alertness. It is a

state of being deeply, peacefully awake. There is the quality of high alertness along with deep peace and a sense of silent presence or stillness. The body is in a state of rest, often deeper than deep sleep. There may also be a sense of boundlessness. We can feel like we live in the eternal Now. The Upanishads call the fourth state Turiya, meaning "the fourth." Yoga calls it Samadhi. As a natural state, it has been experienced and described throughout the ages.

In deep Restful Alertness or samadhi, we settle into consciousness itself, without content. We are simply present and alert with few to no thoughts. This can be called pure consciousness or pure being.

> *Yoga [union] is the complete settling of the activity of the mind. Then the observer is established in their own nature.*
> — Yoga Sutra 1v2-3[2]

One distinct characteristic of a deep samadhi is the automatic stopping of breath. The body and mind have become so quiet that normal breath is not needed. At first this may be noticed as a brief pause. As soon as the mind notices this new experience, it becomes active and the breath resumes. As this deepens, however, such periods can be become extended. We're able to rest in simple awareness and notice it without effort or mental disruption. Then breath can remain paused for half an hour or more. This has been documented with measuring equipment many times by various researchers[3]. When the experience is very clear, we may feel the lungs shift into a fine vibration, just enough to supply the needs of the body.

Such experiences are much more likely to be clear when we're well rested and can go deep, such as on an extended retreat. But they can arise at any time.

Most people have had occasional experiences of profound inner peace or joy or silence, perhaps triggered by the beauty of nature or music or being "in the zone" in sports or during a performance. If the experience doesn't trigger strong emotions, we're less likely to remember it and may even forget it ever arising – until it comes again. Without content, it is hard for the mind to grasp or remember.

And yet this fourth state is natural, arising spontaneously with the right circumstance. It has its own distinct physiology, EEG, and so forth. As such, it is not an "altered" state but turns out to be an essential part of our growth: to discover who we are beneath the ego or me-sense. Without that, is it any wonder our development stalls? How can we expect to grow if we don't even know who we are?

Practice

This brings us to a primary reason for spiritual practice. There is a cornucopia of "spiritual" practices available. Some cities are full of yoga studios that teach exercise rather than Yoga (union), for example. There are also many forms of meditation that bring a variety of benefits. But if they are not bringing the fourth state, they are not leading as directly to post-personal development[4]. Efforts to control the activity of the mind or breath are doing it the hard way.

We also want to be careful we're getting appropriate

instruction. Commonly used mantras like Om culture a renunciate life. Most people will want a householders mantra.

Practices like Mindfulness and Inquiry tend to arise naturally as presence (consciousness) is cultured through the fourth state. But if insufficient presence has been developed, such practices may only be mind referring to itself. The technique becomes another form of personal control.

Guided practices like following a voice are usually a form of hypnosis, something that has benefits but again, not samadhi.

A deep, effortless meditation and related techniques culture the experience of source or essential being. Regular experience of silent presence enlivens it in our experience, bringing the best spiritual progress. It engages personal growth on a much deeper level.

Because that deep peace also creates very deep rest in the physiology, it offers a profound opportunity for healing and purification. A cleaner physiology supports clearer experiences and increased sattva, discussed further along. And critically, it also makes the process smoother subjectively. With enough purification, the openings to our more subtle koshas (Layers, above) will have less to release and offer smoother shifts. This is the point of the practices of many traditions. Having good habits matters.

Even if our subjective experience during the practice is foggy or variable, the deep rest continues to purify and bring progress.

The best practice I know of for this is an effortless mantra meditation like Transcendental Meditation (TM) or similar. TM in particular has an extensive body of research to back it up. Because this is an experiential process, it is best taught by a qualified teacher so that we avoid the mind's tendency to manipulate and get in the way of the practice. It is very common for effort to creep in and interfere. As a result, learning from a book or CD is not usually effective.

I have seen some evidence that related approaches may be key for certain types of people. For example, a more somatic person may find deep silence in effortless asana (postures), but I've not seen equivalent research to establish that. Key is regular samadhi by whatever means we find it.

At first, restful alertness is transcendence, as we go beyond our usual experience and transcend the thinking mind into pure consciousness or yoga. But when it becomes more ongoing, presence becomes a better word. It is ever-present; it is fundamental. There becomes no doubt that consciousness is at the root of all we experience.

This is further illustrated by another detail we may discover. Each time we change states of consciousness, such as from waking to sleep, we briefly go into a neutral gear of consciousness alone. We step from one state to another through the fourth state. All of us experience this multiple times a day. But for most of us, that experience is foggy and brief, unnoticed as it shifts by. But with some purification and resulting clarity, this becomes apparent. I found it most obvious in the morning as I was waking and conscious before the mind-driven concept of a personal self came on-line. For a moment, I was alert but had no sense of me. Then it kicked in, perhaps jolted by not being in control. Again, this points to the fourth state being the ground state of the other three.

In the Yoga Sutra, Patanjali spoke of stages of samadhi. We might call them degrees of clarity and intensity. Keep in mind that silent being or pure consciousness isn't a thing we experience. It is the absence of content. In a day-to-day practice, samadhi is often anything but clear. The fatigue and stress of the day cloud subjectivity. Often, we notice only quiet spells where we settle into the fog. And yet the physiology shows we're transcending, and the benefits develop.

Samadhi can also come with a bang and a great release. That can make a big impression. And that may lead us into chasing the return of such an experience. But the flash and release are just side effects. Experiences are always temporary; they come and go. Experience is not Being. Being or Amness, who we are within, is what we're wanting to culture.

Support

We may also wish to supplement an effortless meditation. Yoga describes 8 limbs, including asana (posture), pranayama (breath), and meditation that together are Raja or royal yoga. The combination can help quality of life and smooth the process.

There are often energetic blockages ("hard nuts") that get in the way of progress by reducing clarity and flow.

We can target healing of energetic issues by using stage 3 energetic literacy (energy reading skills) and issue-appropriate healing skills. These can be learned or we can use a qualified healer[5].

As we make good progress, time with an awake person we resonate with (darshan) can help catalyze shifting. Awakened consciousness in another can stir awakeness within. In person is ideal but live remote can be potent and recordings somewhat as well. Just take care that it's presence you're noticing not charisma.

If we have devotional tendencies, we may find culturing the heart very beneficial. This may include gratitude, surrendering prayer, and a suitable object of devotion. In the Vedic tradition, a suitable object can include one's teacher, a chosen form of God, or one's mate. Just be sure you're not getting drawn into a co-dependent relationship with an unhealed teacher or astral being. Seeking an outside source to meet your needs is not devotion.

With any approach, making moods, avoiding issues, and focusing on appearances offers no value.

This is not a text on techniques though, so I'll leave it there. I go into more detail on my web site[6].

Experiences

There is another detail about experiences that's important to understand. Some people have many experiences associated with higher stages in this process, perhaps shifting into a detached witness or having refined perceptions. But an experience is not it. We can call it a taste but we should not consider a taste more than a shadow. An experience can be quite profound or insightful but is always temporary. Having the scent of fresh bread is not the same as owning the bakery.

Some people have powerful experiences and think, "this is it – I just have to get it back again." This can be deeply limiting as it creates identification with a memory (a past experience) plus expectations of how it "should be." This can keep us trapped in the past rather than making the desired change real.

The key is recognizing the difference between the silence, the experiences it might trigger, and the purification that may happen. Experiences and purification are much more likely to be noticed but are temporary. It is the quiet, silent being to favour. That grows with a good practice and is what leads to awakening.

With a deep enough opening or gradually over time, who we see ourselves as being and who we are in the world will change.

There are large numbers of people in the world today in this Approach phase.

Example Descriptions

> *When I sit to meditate and my awareness sinks into the transcendent, the concerns and worries that may have been gripping my mind fall away, and become supplanted with bliss (sometimes quiet, sometimes bubbly) and peace. The experience is very nourishing... The transcendent is completeness.*
> — anonymous[7]

There sometimes springs an interior peace and quietude which is full of happiness, for the soul is in such a state that it thinks there is nothing that it lacks. Even speaking – by which I mean vocal prayer and meditation – wearies it: it would like to do nothing but love. This condition lasts for some time, and may even last for long periods.
— St. Teresa of Avila[8]

The Observer

Some teachers describe an initial jiva or soul awakening into presence before the first post-personal stage. This is less common but not unusual. A key aspect of supporting an awakening in the physiology is a rise of energy from the root of the spine up through the chakras to the crown of the head. This energy is known as kundalini (coiled), then as kundalini Shakti (energy) as it rises. While I'll explore further shortly, a few points are useful to understand the mechanics of this stage. When the kundalini Shakti rises above the throat chakra, the observer or sense of detached witness comes on-line. We no longer experience ourselves as the body-mind but rather as a simple observer of them. (recall the 3-fold nature of consciousness above)

The first [stage] is realization of Self Consciousness.
— Maharishi Mahesh Yogi[9]

This is not a disassociative state, nor is it a spacey state of dreamy escapism. It is a very solid, grounded state of being where we take a step back into our deeper nature prior to the mind.

Some people may get the impression of an "awakening" at this point. However, the kundalini Shakti is still variable so it drops again, either quickly or after a time. When it drops, the witness goes away and the experience is lost. We fall back into our old sense of self.

But if the kundalini Shakti pierces the last "cap" and reaches a point called Makara, just above the 6th chakra ("third eye"), she no longer drops but becomes stable. Then the observer becomes ongoing. We are the detached observer through all the other states of consciousness.

The distance from Makara to Bindu at the top of the head and awakening is small. However, for some people, the process pauses there to better prepare the physiology. If that is the case, the person finds themselves as a witness to their lives but not quite Self-Realized.

Turning on the witness is a very distinct shift, creating a continuity of awareness underlying the states of waking, sleeping, and dreaming. A part of us is ever-present and never "sleeps" again. The body and mind sleep but consciousness does not. This can be verified with EEG: in witnessing sleep, the alpha frequencies of alertness are overlaid on the delta of deep sleep.

But being conscious doesn't mean experiencing. In witnessing sleep, we may watch the body fall asleep and become immobile. But as long as there is experiencing taking place, the mind is still active. It is not yet full sleep. In deep sleep, we drop into the timeless silence. That part of the night zooms by with no experience. Yet a continuity of Self remains throughout all states[10].

Witnessing may be associated with Self Realization,

the first post-personal stage. Maharishi described the witnessing of deep sleep as a key symptom of Cosmic Consciousness (Self Realization). But it can arise prior to that shift. I know several people, including myself, who witnessed for decades before their actual awakening. The key is that they have recognized the Self (Atman) within but they are still identified with the ego or sense of "me." It is not yet post-personal. We can describe it as non-local but not yet infinite. The Self has not woken up to Itself through the apparent person yet. It has been recognized but we have not "become" it yet. Self is conscious but it has not yet been Realized. We are not liberated. We'll go into this more in the Self Realization section.

There are several well-known spiritual teachers who consider themselves awake but seem to be in this range. It is very easy to confuse witnessing with awakening, and the ego may grasp such an experience and inflate the self-sense.

In spite of the caveats, this is a platform for faster development because of ongoing presence. There is a quality of samadhi that has become ongoing, though not as deep as Self Realization.

Example Descriptions

Often during deep sleep I am awake inside, in a very peaceful, blissful state. Dreams come and go, thoughts about the dreams come and go, but I remain in a deeply peaceful state, completely free from the dreams and the thoughts. My body is asleep and inert, breathing goes on regularly and mechanically, and inside I am just aware that I am.

Something inside me doesn't go to sleep... My attention softly goes within. I become less and less aware of my surroundings, I become less and less aware of thoughts. At some point, all melts away. I stop experiencing everything except pure clarity. It's crystal clear alertness inside. Time doesn't exist. The light never goes out deep within... If I didn't have dreams I might think I'd never fallen completely asleep, because the inner alertness is so strong...
— anonymous[12]

In my case, after several brief periods of witnessing, the Shakti reached makara with a blinding white flash and I began witnessing full-time during an extended retreat in the mid-1970's. For the first few days, I was hyper-vigilant, watching the body fall asleep and turn into an immovable lump. I was also thinking about the experience and manipulating dreams. But soon I realized I could just relax into it and fully allow the process. It later became clear that if I was thinking about the experience, then mind wasn't asleep. In deep sleep, even the mind and ego-sense slept and there was simply quiet being. That continuity of awareness has never ended. I didn't come and go with waking and sleep but was always present. The actual awakening took place quite a few years later.

Higher Stages of Development

The post-personal Stages are shifts in our relationship with consciousness and its clarity. While we might say "stages of consciousness," consciousness itself doesn't develop. What is shifting is the clarity and depth of consciousness at a point of observation, our local aspect of the whole.

It's important to understand these are post-personal stages. The individual person does not become enlightened. Consciousness, the higher Self or atman, is what is discovering these higher perspectives and greater fullness of Itself. The sense of individuality takes a progressively smaller role.

However, this doesn't mean the person ends or we cease having a human life. Enlightenment is not an escape from our humanity. Instead, our universal nature becomes more prominent and our perspective evolves substantially.

While the experience of this process varies widely for many reasons, there are common distinct stages that happen as Consciousness becomes more awake to its own totality. Each stage also has degrees of clarity. Thus, an apparent process occurs as Consciousness unfolds to Itself here. We might compare this to puberty. Puberty is experienced a wide range of ways but has a common underlying process.

These stages are each quite distinct because each one changes our global sense of reality. How we experience, understand, and perceive the world and ourselves are altered. If the shift is unclear, that is not yet it or it's not yet established. Time will tell.

This approach is a blend derived from the Yog Vasishtha. This text is the core teaching from the sage Vasishtha, given to Rama in the royal court during the epic story Ramayana. Based on astronomical references, estimates place these events over 8,000 years ago. My interpretation originates with Maharishi Mahesh Yogi's and is further informed by Lorne Hoff, the study of Vedic science, and the experience of this process by various people, including myself. I have also included elements from Ayurveda, Kundalini traditions, Zen, Tantra, and modern energy modalities.

The Two Aspects

In Ayurveda, the medicine of the Vedas, they suggest we're born with six bhavas (houses or aspects). Three of them relate to our family of origin and three to what we bring forward from prior lifetimes. This includes prior spiritual development. This is why we see the occasional person who makes rapid progress after little practice or awakens with no apparent history. Their history was likely prior, although anything is possible.

The two bhavas of particular interest here are Atman and Sattva. Atman refers to consciousness and the degree of silent being (presence) developed – the awakeness or alertness of consciousness to itself.

Sattva is purity or clarity, our inner light. It relates to the lively quality of consciousness* and the degree of refinement of perception. We could say it is clarity of consciousness but also clarity of the various layers (koshas) described previously. It is clarity of the intellect, the mind, the heart, and so forth. We recognize this clarity by growing perception of those layers.

(* alertness and liveliness are two fundamental qualities of consciousness. I'll come back to this later.)

Some traditions emphasize consciousness while others emphasize sattva.

Someone with more sattva will have more refined perception of both the physical world and more subtle values. They may have more sensitivity, remarkable experiences, and fine feelings. Yet they may or may not be skilled with them. Less atman and they will not be as grounded in being and may find normal life challenging – they are too easily caught and tossed by huge experiences.

Someone with more atman established will have deep meditations and be less caught by experiences. More atman and less sattva means more presence but less refinement and less of a connection between the outer world and their inner being. Thus, they may describe more detachment, less heart, and a drier, flatter unfoldment. Emptiness rather than fullness. Atman is required for the key permanent shifts, but sattva is what fills it out.

Some teaching discourages sattva, emphasizing detached consciousness. And some teachings promote sattva without the grounding of consciousness. From my perspective, the ideal is both, in balance, not seeking experiences but allowing life to unfold and educating yourself in both being and the worlds you live in – those koshas again.

These two, atman and sattva, are also described in the literature as the male and female aspects, e.g., Shiva and Shakti or Yang and Yin.

Later in the process, we move beyond consciousness

and thus beyond both atman and sattva. However, the process of increasing clarity and purity continues indefinitely.

Notes

1 New International version

2 Egenes translation (2010), see Bibliography

3 Breath suspension during meditation, research examples: ncbi.nlm.nih.gov/pubmed/7045911
ncbi.nlm.nih.gov/pubmed/6377350

4 drfredtravis.com/downloads/Travis_preprint.pdf

5 rose-rosetree.com

6 davidya.ca

7 The Supreme Awakening p 52 , from Creating Heaven on Earth, section 2:6

8 Spiritual Relations, as quoted in The Supreme Awakening p107

9 Commentary on the Bhagavad Gita, Ch6 v47

10 davidya.ca/2017/04/04/witnessing-sleep

11 The Supreme Awakening p186

12 The Supreme Awakening p185

The Overview

Be still
Stillness reveals the secrets of eternity
Eternity embraces the all-possible
The all-possible leads to a vision of oneness
A vision of oneness brings about universal love
Universal love supports the great truth of Nature
The great truth of Nature is Tao

Whoever knows this truth lives forever
The body may perish, deeds may be forgotten
But he who has Tao has all eternity."
— Tao Te Xhing, v16[1]

The two aspects I mentioned above, atman and sattva, intertwine as two sides of the larger process.

The first aspect, Atman (consciousness), unfolds in three primary Stages of Consciousness awakening to Itself. First it awakens to itself within, then to itself in the world, and then to its origins beyond itself. Each stage begins with a deep realization or shift in being. Each has many possible sub-stages and variations in how it is experienced subjectively.

The Stages:
1) Self Realization / Cosmic Consciousness
2) Unity Consciousness / Oneness / Non-duality
3) Beyond Consciousness / Brahman

There is NOT a single awakening that matures into fully flowered enlightenment. Rather, there are three key shifts, each with their own distinct sense of self and reality. The truth of one stage is not the truth of another. This is why it's important to understand what any given teacher is speaking about – the context determines the truth. This will become clear as we explore the stages in detail.

When I use the term "Realization," I am referring to a sense of becoming, a recognition on the level of our very existence that changes our sense of who we are. This is not a conceptual "aha" or an idea or feeling. It is beyond the mind. In fact, when it happens the mind is often disoriented and at a loss for words for a time.

These are not "altered states" of consciousness. It is a stage of development in consciousness itself. A temporary experience of some of this may have an altered feel. But the actual shift is the discovery of who you've always been, a recognition of consciousness by itself.

The other side of this coin is Sattva: the refinement of the physiology; the awakening of the heart; and the progressively greater embodiment of the awakenings above. The mechanism for refinement is mostly soma, discussed in more detail further along. Refinement is a continuous process that may begin long before the stages above or become apparent long after. However, each time there is a stage change, the context for the refinement changes, bringing a new experience of it.

> *This morning, outside I stood*
> *I saw a little red-winged bird*
> *Shining like a burning bush*
> *Singing like a scripture verse*
> *It made me want to bow my head...*
> *Everything is holy now*
> — Peter Mayer, from the song *Holy Now*[2]

Thus, each stage has its own refined version: refined Cosmic Consciousness; refined Unity; and refined Brahman. Unlike the stages in consciousness, these do not begin with a shift in being (realization) but rather have their realizations at the climax, prior to the next shift in consciousness.

Because of the dominance of mind over heart in Western culture, many people have developed less refinement and thus there is much less recognition of this process in current spiritual circles. This is partly why you see little talk of devas (light beings), celestial perception, the divine, and so forth in many "awakened" communities. Some teachers even discount it as false or delusional. Ken Wilber, for example, described the subject as a mythic throwback to a bygone era. But denying a whole swath of direct experience is not helpful. That can lead to confusion and repression.

It's not uncommon for people whose perception flowers to realize they had glimpses in their early life (due to prior development) but were actively discouraged and learned to suppress it.

The Post-Personal Stages in Summary
1) Self Realization / Cosmic Consciousness
1a) God Consciousness / Refined Cosmic Consciousness
2) Unity Consciousness / Oneness / Non-duality
2a) Refined Unity and God Realization
3) Beyond Consciousness / Brahman
3a) Refined Brahman
3b) ParaBrahman / Pure Divinity

A few things to note about this model:

The 7 States model that I mentioned in the opening includes the first three to Unity although Maharishi spoke of all of these at different points.

It's also worth noting that this is an organic process. Every person's shift varies subjectively, including the degree of clarity. It is very rare for someone to have a single complete realization of any of these stages in one go. Usually we open the door, step into the shift, then gradually increase clarity and discover what is now here. Over time, there is more clearing, the clarity deepens, and the shift is integrated and embodied. But teachers are noticing a trend to smoother and deeper transitions as it becomes more common.

The body's endocrine system also needs to mature (around age 24) to support integrating this process. If the body is still growing, the platform is not yet stable. In prior historical ages, the post-personal stages were said to naturally unfold during the mid to late 20's. Enlightenment was normal in prior golden ages, and refinement progressed over many years.

Finally, if you are comparing this model to others, be careful they're describing the same range. I've seen multi-staged models using higher stage terminology but describing earlier soul awakening prior to post-personal development. There are also well-known models like the Buddhist Ten Bulls[3] that describe stages in the approach to Self Realization, the bull being the ego. The steps are describing success with the practice.

I've not adopted such approaches as I've not found consistent steps other than what I've listed in The Approach section above. There are many possible sub-steps that will vary by person and not everyone will experience. There are also models that describe the process of a different time that is not as relevant now, like Kaivalya (singularity) in Yoga. It is the singularity that awakens to the whole but in this age, we don't tend to recognize this until late Unity.

The Energy Process

There are various ways traditions describe the energy shifts taking place that support embodying this awakening process. How we experience this will vary by the condition of our physiology, the techniques we practice, the kinds of things there are to release, and how we relate to it. Further, much of it remains very subtle and out of awareness.

The common understanding is a kundalini awakening in the root of the spine with Shakti rising up through the spine (sushumna nadi) and chakras to the crown and awakening. Shakti rises to join Shiva (observer aspect of consciousness).

What then follows is the descent of Grace, of Shiva and Shakti together, through a higher octave of the original 7 chakras (described prior).

This aligns with my interpretation of the *Kundalini Vidya* tradition, as described by Joan Harrigan, PhD[4]. Self Realization happens when the kundalini reaches the crown chakra. Then, through "advanced process," Shiva and Shakti descend together through the chakras, awakening more subtle values. These correspond to the further stages mentioned above – head (1), heart (1a), solar plexus (2) and root (3).

This also aligns with Zen's Adyashanti, describing "head, heart, gut"[5] and his conversation with Loch Kelly in *Journey After Awakening*[6]. And it aligns with the Vedic approach of Maharishi Mahesh Yogi, as seen in one of his rare talks on the subject[7]:

> *The Kundalini finds its absorption in all these centres... and eventually here in the cortex... a thousand-petaled lotus.*

> *And by the time Kundalini comes here, everything, the whole thing becomes full of light. Full of light means full of awareness. Light means not this light, but pure Being. And when this whole area becomes aware of Being clearly, then it is Cosmic Consciousness.*

When Shakti completes the descent that follows, *Kundalini Vidya* describes a rising again to a chakra based on the needs of this embodiment. We may also describe a second rise related to embodying pure Divinity late in this process. However, I've seen various other styles like a second, larger descent related to Shiva. This may relate to the dominance of Shiva or Shakti, be subjective variations, or be other processes I've not seen mapped.

A basic model of the resulting process would be the kundalini awakening, a rise through three "caps" (blocks to be pierced) and other sundry debris to the crown and awakening. Then a descent through head, heart, gut, root, followed by a final rise into Divinity. But there can be great variation in emphasis in various individual experiences. For example, the 2nd chakra may be prominent in refined Unity or the throat chakra when bliss comes online.

Yet not all traditions describe the process this way.

There is a second group of traditions that don't describe a formal rise at all. Instead, they describe a circulation of the vayus (airs, prana) clearing the channels (nadis), then a descent of grace.

But as Harrigan points out in *Kundalini Vidya*, mantra meditators are inclined to notice little in the way of obvious kundalini experiences until the rise reaches the third eye and the lights come on.

Some traditions, including the Christian, consider this ideal as it is smoother and less associated with physiological issues. Sri Aurobindo evidently also favoured this.

If this is the experience, we may well relate to this second style of describing it. But I suspect the rise and descent approach is a more complete understanding. I'm not one of the rare ones who have a Chitrini rising[8] (within Sushumna) and experience full detail, but the first matches what I've seen better.

A third perspective sees several stages during the initial rise. I've seen this described in various ways with awakening at the gut or the heart, climaxing with Unity at the crown. I understand this is what the Kashmir Shaivism tradition describes. After Shakti rises to the crown, it is said to descend to the heart via the amrita channel. It takes the mind with it, dissolving the mind in the heart for a full embodiment. This puts the heart descent I mentioned above in a different context.

A way we might integrate this style of experience is that perhaps Shiva sometimes descends to meet Shakti part way up. Thus the awakening, the meeting of Shiva and Shakti, occurs at a lower chakra. Or it may simply be a variation in how it is subjectively being experienced. I've seen alternative explanations for several key events.

Some report their "awakening" at other centres or align the stages at different points of descent. And I've seen variations like a concurrent rise and descent. But if these are unique subjective variations, they may not help illustrate the normal process.

This variety makes one thing clear. The energetic process is not the underlying mechanism but rather the physiology's adaptation to a deeper shift taking place behind all that. Broadly though, we know there is purification, opening, and refinement taking place on all levels while the koshas (layers) are prepared for, then adapting to, unfolding awareness.

We can describe this process as energetic embodiment of the shifts in consciousness.

Whatever chakra we're identified with when the rise begins, when it passes this point it will draw our attention and development upwards.

We can see that most of our subjective experiences revolve around the body, energy (emotional) changes, and perceptions. These involve just the grossest three layers (koshas). Much of the causal process takes place out of our clear experiential range. *Kundalini Vidya* tells us the crown chakra manages the openings of the lower chakras and nadis (energy channels). But as the crown itself doesn't have sensations, we are commonly only aware of the lower effects rather than the whole process.

Intensity

Some may experience the initial rise as almost unnoticeable, like the mantra meditators mentioned above – just some occasional movements or sensations (kriyas) here and there in the body from clearing. Or there may be little to notice – if someone had their initial rise in a prior lifetime, they won't have it again this time. They'll pick up where they left off, so there won't be another "kundalini awakening."

Some may notice the process more and some may find it quite intense, perhaps even require some support for managing it.[9]

Some instructors teach intense breathing exercises and other techniques to encourage a rise or even try to push it. This approach is more likely to be intense, even violent. I would consider this playing with fire. Kundalini opens naturally of its own accord if we culture samadhi as discussed before. This is a much smoother, more natural path. Should it happen to come on strongly anyway, that's when kundalini techniques and certain asanas (yoga postures) can be very valuable to soothe or redirect the fire.

Deflected Risings

Kundalini Vidya notes that some kinds of traumatic experiences like torture or extreme sexual experiences, even in a prior lifetime, can cause kundalini energy to become "deflected" and rise up a secondary channel rather than the central Sushumna. This kind of deflected rising can bring on various things like charisma, talents, brilliance, and profound experiences. Such a person may even become a sought after spiritual teacher. However, in such secondary channels the kundalini is unstable and rises and falls, causing a kind of energetic bipolar problem. These secondary channels also do not reach the top so stable kundalini and an awakening are not possible.

I've met a couple of these, one claiming he went straight into Unity, then later saying he "battled the gods" to undo his enlightenment. As the gods don't give us enlightenment, they can't take it away either.

This is a complex subject that requires expert analysis

to diagnose[10]. The solution requires bringing the energy down and redirecting it up the correct channel. But it's worth being aware of this as some charismatic "awakened" people are just riding the energy.

You may also run into "instant enlightenment" gurus with flashy experiences and abilities that are still very much ego-identified and may be unstable. Such people can be very attractive but tend to leave a wake of wounded people. They are not who you should follow.

Exceptions

Sometimes people seem to skip past some of the stages. They can happen quickly, one after the other, like the witness coming on-line then awakening. If there is little separation, they may not be experienced as distinct. But usually there is a bit of time between the major stages.

About the fastest I've seen is three days between major stages, but usually it's months or years. And that's a good thing. It's much better for a new stage to be built on the stable platform of an integrated prior stage. A fast series can require quite a bit of time to integrate later.

One variation that may encourage very rapid unfolding is that possibility of having an awakening in a prior lifetime but not finishing the process. The opportunity may arise to finish it now. Such a person would tend to fly though the stages already met or even seem to be born awake. However, the physiology would usually need to mature and stabilize before it fills out.

Due to Western culture, it's not unusual to skip the refined stages until later on. The physiology simply doesn't meet the required refinement for them to unfold yet. When there is enough clarity, they will begin to be noticed from the context of whatever stage is then lived.

Much more common is someone using higher language to describe their experience, like mistaking inner oneness for non-duality. Or confusing jiva awakening with Self Realization. People also often use the term Brahman for presence or consciousness. Mariana Caplan explores the issue in her book *Halfway Up The Mountain: The Error of Premature Claims to Enlightenment.*

Someone who shifts without a spiritual history is more likely to notice spacious emptiness, perhaps with a sense of illusory world. Without a momentum of spiritual practice, they may mature in place without further stages. Nothing is skipped but no further stages unfold.

We may run into someone having a deflected kundalini rising with lots of flashy experiences and charisma but no actual awakening, as noted above. Such examples are energy-driven rather than a shift in being so will fail at some point.

Perhaps someone will frame their experience quite differently, in a way that is incompatible with a stages-in-consciousness approach. I've met a few who could not relate to this approach, even though it was clear to me they were progressing through this process. They may relate better to one of the other models I mentioned near the beginning, even if it's not as inclusive.

Verification

Your best verification is time and the embodiment of each stage. Often, a shift can have variable clarity for a time. But as you get further into the process, clarity dawns and makes it largely self-verifying. It is useful to have external verification of the first shift though, as it is very new territory.

There are points in a journey where we may find it helpful to speak with someone with a similar process who has been there before. They can help clarify points of confusion, perhaps also give a language for the mind to digest what has happened. A little clarity can speed up the integration process.

This is partly why study of the old texts has been historically recommended. But after a shift, we often have to toss out our old understanding and reexamine teachings in light of direct experience. This is like going to another country for the first time. We may have studied it extensively but the actual experience will be a surprise. Even *Google Street View* isn't the same as being there.

The Zen tradition has a long history of tests for "enlightenment." Generally, these are testing for effects, like equanimity and compassion. The various branches of Buddhism have developed widely variable definitions of enlightenment. A single teaching can describe the stages into Self Realization while also describing an advanced standard of perfection that is very rare.

As these shifts become more common, other styles of verification are becoming available.

Brain EEG can verify witnessing deep sleep is occurring as alpha frequencies are overlaid on the delta of sleep described prior. Deep samadhi can also be confirmed.

Rose Rosetree[11], an energy healer and teacher, helps people develop "energetic literacy" (subtle perception) through books, coaching, and workshops. She indicates that everyone can learn to read the energy body. With "stage 3" energetic literacy, you can read enough to recognize the characteristics of energy clarity in others, the sattva side of the process. She indicates someone who has balanced chakra databanks, is quite clear of energetic dross, and has divine presence has the energetic markers of enlightenment.

However, she does distinguish this from an awakening in consciousness. Someone awake may not yet be clear of dross nor have established a clear divine connection. They would not meet her standard yet. But someone who has a clear energy physiology but has not yet awoken in consciousness would read as enlightened.

The other systems I've seen that use energy readings are deficient.

For any verification system – the key to look at is what are they verifying? The effects of an actual shift? Or secondary things that may or may not point to a shift? We need to choose ones that are true adaptations.

Keep in mind that we don't awaken because kundalini

rose to the crown or the energy is clear. Awakening in consciousness is much deeper than this. We awaken because Self wakes up to itself through this apparent form. The form then adapts to the shift. If it cannot support or embody the shift yet, there will be a temporary experience that will fade, without a change in being.

Notes

1 Jonathan Star translation (2003)

2 youtu.be/KiypaURysz4

3 en.wikipedia.org/wiki/Ten_Bulls

4 See Bibliography

5 Adyashanti, *Emptiness Dancing* (2006)

6 adyashanti.org DVD: *Journey After Awakening*

7 Lake Louise, 1968

8 See *Kundalini Vidya* in Bibliography

9 kundalinicare.com

10 kundalinicare.com

11 rose-rosetree.com

Part Two

The Stages in Detail

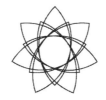

Stage 1
Self Realization

I stood at rest in the midst of the world.
— Jesus, The Gospel of Thomas 28

Also known as Cosmic Consciousness, this first shift is profoundly simple. It is not an experience but a permanent change in being. But as we have no reference point for it and are so used to looking outside into experience, we miss it. It may come with experiences or purification, but that is not the actual shift.

It is not a thought or idea. That's mind.
It is not something we can understand until it is lived. Before that, it's just an idea.
It is not a peak experience or altered state.
It is not an experience we once had and remember.
It is not something the person will gain or achieve. The shift takes place beyond the person.
It is not just an ongoing witness or observer.

Actual Self Realization occurs when that inner wakefulness or observer (presence or pure consciousness) awakens to or remembers itself cosmically. We may or may not have already recognized ourselves as consciousness (Being, I Am), but the realization happens in either case. It is a profound shift in our sense of being, in the sense of who we are. The "I" is no longer localized in an individual body-mind but rather is expansive awareness observing through the body-mind. We are the cosmic witness, unbound from a personal sense of self. This is the beginning of the post-personal process.

> *Freedom has nothing to do with experiences. It is found in a moment of silence, in a simple knowing that everything is okay the way it is, in a moment of resting, in what is not of this body/mind and in the recognition of stillness in the midst of everything happening.*
> — Neelam[1]

The shift is characterized by a sense of boundless freedom and liberation. We find cosmic being underlies all things and we are everywhere present. There is a deep inner peace. The shift will not come and go (although its clarity might) but will have key features and will mature over time.

Framed another way, the coming and going of the state of Presence Consciousness shifts into being the ground state of all experience. We are Presence itself. This is Turiyatita, "beyond the fourth" (state).

For some, this shift is clear and unmistakable, especially if there has been a history of witnessing. For others, the shift can be less clear and take some time to become established. And for others, there can be a glimpse but it's not sustained if the physiology is not quite ready.

If the shift is unclear for various reasons, we can't say it's fully present. Many fall back into the mind for a time while they wind down resistance or clear energetically. Adyashanti calls this "non-abiding[2]."

It's very difficult to personally distinguish an unclear shift from a passing glimpse or from being unable to sustain an opening. It's best to give it time and see what lasts. It can help to have the support of an experienced teacher also.

If there has been the shift, it will become clear over time as the impediments to clarity fall away.

Release

The shift itself is often accompanied by purification and various experiences. It's common to laugh or cry or both with the accompanying release. Typically, there is some sense of a deeper letting go but it may take a more specific form. There may be a sense of a "last stress" or "last barrier" falling prior to the shift. For example, there may be a sense of letting go of a key concept of how this is "supposed to" appear.

Similarly, some may experience the release or healing of a deep wound prior to the shift. Because of its personal subjective importance, it may be elevated to a "core wound." But this is unlikely to be the last healing, so its status may be over-emphasized. We certainly shouldn't expect a traumatic release, though there is often some purification.

The shift may also be accompanied by a high level of contrast. That newness will quickly fade, leaving the actual shift unchanged.

It's key to recognize that the shift itself is not an experience. It is a change in the experiencer, in who we recognize ourselves to be. The release and flash will end. The awakening is under that and is what remains when the dust settles. We must be careful not to confuse the effects with the cause. Other descriptions often mention the phenomena as that's easier to describe. But that is not the shift itself.

Integration

It usually takes time to adapt to this shift and become established. We have been living for so long identified with the surface of life, overshadowed by the mind and senses. Now we are awakening from that fog. Soon the shift becomes unshakable or "abiding", as Adyashanti has put it. Then we have the first stage of Enlightenment. The kindergarten, as we may later call it.

With the shift, existing practices like meditation can become quite different. Who is meditating? In my case, for example, the person who used to meditate was now off in the infinite distance. How was there to be a practice? But in a few days, things integrated better. The body-mind aligned with this point of observation. Now there was no longer a "going within" because I was already there. Meditation became more a settling out of the mind and body into silent peace.

Some think the need for practices is now done. With the fall of the seeker, we can *feel* done. However, this results from the idea that practices are for awakening or for the seeker. But if we instead understand that practices are for refinement, there is much more to be done. The practices may evolve, but they should continue. I've seen some beneficially begin an effortless meditation practice *after* they woke up.

The Yoga Sutra describes liberation as Kaivalya, the singularity. This is from the higher perspective of the point of observation recognizing its global nature. In the current time, that knowing doesn't usually arise until late Unity. We'll explore this in the Unity section later.

Trauma Trigger

Much of what I frame here is based on someone who pursues a spiritual path. However, there are cases where a major trauma triggers an ego-collapse and resulting opening. For this to take place, there has to be sufficient clarity pre-existing or the opening will not occur. But if there is, people can shift straight out of a personal hell into surprising clarity. Eckhart Tolle[3] and Byron Katie[4] would be well-known examples.

Because of the circumstances of such a shift, they have no context for the change. This may lead to confusion about what has occurred. It's more likely for it to be experienced as a falling away of the person into an emptiness. Integrating the change can be much more challenging and may be resisted. Yet their former sense of self is not recovered. Tolle famously spent two years sitting on a park bench in London[5]. In his case he was saturated with bliss and not very functional.

I've noticed there is a tendency to stay with this shift rather than progress as much, perhaps because of the lack of spiritual momentum. But this may also be related to not knowing there is more nor how to culture it.

As I noted in a prior section, another variation on this is a deflected rising. Here, trauma triggers a rising through a secondary side channel that may lead to flashy experiences, charisma, and so forth but not a true awakening.

Variations

Aside from being clear or not, or flashy or not, the shift itself may be described in several ways.

5 Variations in Awakening

1) a falling away of the ego or sense of "me" and a shift into cosmic Self, fullness, or being

2) the same falling away of the ego, but into a "no-self" or emptiness

3) a sense of expanding from an individual self into cosmic or universal Self

4) a devotional surrender into divine being

5) a quiet shift that clarifies over time. One "oozes" forward and may not notice a distinct shift.

You may have noticed these variations can be a little confusing. Some of the above sound like very different things: awakening to fullness vs. awakening to emptiness, for example. But these are subjective differences in the experience of it, not a different thing. And yet, the later Brahman shift into "nothing" can sound like emptiness but is completely different. If we're going to discriminate effectively, we need to understand these distinctions.

An expansive experience of feeling boundless and free might be described as an awakening but is an experience, not a change in the experiencer (being). Some experiences will even change our sense of who we are. But the actual awakening being described is the shift in being (consciousness) rather than an experience.

As may be obvious, the mind alone cannot interpret this properly. But these distinctions can be very useful for someone having the unfolding.

When people describe this as a shift to "no-self" (#2 above), this may be due to the terminology of their tradition, such as Buddhism. Or it may be due to a lack of clarity. We can notice a falling away of the me without recognizing what we're becoming instead. In the examples I know, that clarity came over time.

When the shift is clear, the change can be distinct enough that our past sense of self is suddenly seen through as a false illusion. Some may even have a sense of an "ego death." It can certainly seem for a time that the ego is gone. Some renunciate teachings may encourage that. But what really dies is the identification with that sense of individuality. It is no longer who we know ourselves to be, but the function remains. Our own uniqueness and body-mind continues. This point is clarified in the Inflation section shortly.

During the awakening, the light is said to roast mountains of our unresolved backlog (karma). It can be like the center of the story of a me is blown out, leaving shattered remnants of what we once believed about ourselves. That "shrapnel" then arises through life experiences and is resolved quickly and over time.

The mind may try to defend this long-protected narrative. But when the shift is clear enough, we've seen through the stories we once believed and we no longer buy into them. We let them go. The mind becomes much more settled when it no longer has to defend its beliefs.

If there is high sattva (clarity) and a softening of the me-sense from spiritual practice, the shift can be very gentle with less contrast, less sense of identity loss, and perhaps less of a transcendent phase. We simply slide in.

I've seen a few people whose shift was so quiet and natural that they didn't even recognize they were awake.

More typically there is something distinct about the shift: a release, accompanying experiences, or shift in self-sense.

Some may experience a sense of being reborn or born anew. The Vedic texts occasionally refer to someone awake as being twice-born.

It is common for the normalcy and ordinariness of the shift to come as a surprise as well as the recognition of the profound simplicity of it. Why did I not "get" this sooner? There is often a recognition we've been it all along; now we've remembered.

Once the shift is more integrated and the newness overshadowing the old fades, we find that a person with preferences and personality is still there. But it is no longer the center. Who we are has shifted to our cosmic Self (Atman, pure being, pure consciousness, presence). Thus there is a sense of change in who "I" am.

There are also many other words people might use around this. The point here is to develop a useful framework. If we know the key markers, then we can "translate" other terms.

The Quality or Guna

One common change in experience is that the world is now seen as illusory and not-Self. By this I don't mean conceptually but in the direct experience. This can be a flip in our sense of reality. Before, the outer world was real and the inner world changeable and uncertain. Now the inner world is eternal and real and the outer world illusory. This change can be very distinct or quite subtle.

However, this commonly described sense of world-as-illusion is a mode of perception. The mode depends on our dominant guna rather than the stage in consciousness. The guna gives a quality to the awakening but is not the marker that some make it to be. For example, a shift in dominant guna can happen prior to awakening.

A person having more sattva guna will experience the

process itself more directly, will recognize the process is being guided by grace, and may recognize sages and devas (light beings) that are supporting them through the process. Sattva is much more likely to lead to smoother shifts.

Such people will also have the bliss arise more quickly, a much fuller experience, and typically have a clear God Consciousness stage next. The world is seen more as Lila, the divine play, though this may come on after the shift is more established. This underscores why I spoke earlier of the value of developing sattva as well.

When rajas (fire) guna is more dominant, we get the world-as-illusion effect. Ideally, this occurs as heat to burn off the old rigidity (inertia) and release more energy for healing and transformation. This can be necessary to embody the awakening more fully.

But it may also amplify desires, create excess thinking, and cause heat imbalances. Self-importance can be inflated with a premature desire to guide and teach others. (see Inflation)

Rajas also tends to lead to drier forms of awakening with less refinement. Further, until the way is clearer, there can be a delay in the bliss coming on.

Less commonly, there can be a tamas (inertia) style of awakening. Here the process is shadowed by inertia and leads to rigidity, intolerance, or fundamentalism. This style can even show up as a "demonic" type. There are a few examples in the epic stories of old. It can take some real support to shift this process with the "fire of knowledge" and transform the guna. Happily, this is a less common style due to sattvic spiritual practices.

Note that this isn't a black and white thing. All of us are a blend of the gunas. We'll have aspects of each and variations in emphasis as the process unfolds. We'll all have some tamas to burn and rajas to settle.

The Honeymoon

After the shift, there can be what Adyashanti describes as a "honeymoon[6]," a period where the contrast and richness of the shift are enjoyed. Then what has yet to be resolved becomes more prominent. Adyashanti describes the mind trying to reassert itself for a time while what remains (the vasana or impressions) is wound down. He suggests this can take from six months to ten years post-awakening to complete. It depends on what was not resolved prior to the shift or roasted in the fire of the shift itself.

> *Something awake and something in the process of awakening.*
> — Loch Kelly[7]

It also depends on how willing we are to cooperate with the process. If enlightenment is idealized or we've been avoiding our shadow for a long time, this may come home to roost now.

> *If you believe the misperception that enlightenment is only about happiness, bliss, and freedom, you will be motivated to transcend or escape those areas of your life that feel less than fully functional. But sooner or later, as we become more awake, we find that there is more and more pressure to encounter and deal with those areas of*

our lives that we have been avoiding, where we are less than fully conscious.
— Adyashanti, *The End of Your World*

Yet some may move on to higher stages, meaning a yet higher perspective, while the baggage is still being unloaded. And unload it must. The key here is recognizing that the process, like all human development, takes time. Maturity doesn't come overnight. And a grand vision does not a teacher make.

Theres a point at which you're willing to be seen.
— Gangaji[8]

Adyashanti calls this coming completely out of hiding[9].

These levels are not just transcendent of humanness, but also right within your humanness, because there is no separation between your human being and your divine being.

…as we get into the more mature opening of realization, there is no more room for denial.

This is not about perfection; it is about wholeness. It is not about having things exactly as we want them, but about having things exactly as they are. When we allow things to be, a sense of harmony develops; the gap between our realization and who we are as a human being gets smaller and smaller. A seamless continuum begins to emerge between realization and expression, awakening and its actualization.

In fact, the spiritual process isn't any different before

awakening than afterward. It's just that, after awakening, the process is happening from a different perspective; you may think of it as a bird's-eye view versus a ground-level view.
— Adyashanti, *The End of Your World*

One of the oft-mentioned features of liberation is the end of reincarnation and our repeated return to the school of karma. But awakening alone doesn't do the job. While we may roast much of our backlog, it's the follow-up unpacking and resolution of our history that winds down the "wheel of karma" and completes that process.

After this, the soul is said to have the choice to merge with source or continue in a higher arena, perhaps in a supporting role.

This highlights the value of healing and good techniques. They are not for awakening itself but rather for upgrading the vessel so our experience of life is optimized and our awakening is as smooth and as clear as possible. These comments should also clarify the fact that we don't have to be perfect and pure to awaken, not even slightly. But it can certainly help if we're supporting the process. Meditation, good lifestyle, and the company of the wise can really help with a quality awakening into the fullness of who we are.

There are texts that describe a maturing of enlightenment to take 12 years. I would not consider that a fixed rule, but it gives you an idea of the time it takes living life to integrate and embody these changes.

Inflation

Closely related to the mind reasserting itself post-awakening is the issue of inflation. Ego has had a long habit of claiming experiences as "mine," and it's common for some of this to creep back in – even if we felt an "ego death." Ego claims my enlightenment, my specialness, my vision, my importance, and so forth. We may over-estimate our progress and integration. We may feel beyond others or that no one else can understand our reality.

This is more common with dominant rajas, discussed prior. If the person has experienced the variation where their ego expanded to become cosmic, the problem can be more overt but also obvious. When the claiming is more subtle, it can be unrecognized. But if we understand the ego remains, we can be alert to its machinations.

A feeling of satisfaction and pride is perfectly normal when mixed in with the relief of awakening. Just remember where that's coming from. We're so used to ego's involvement that we don't notice it's there. We may think "I always question my assumptions" but what is questioning what? The ego can make great displays of its thoughtful neutrality while it plays criminal, prosecutor, and judge.

Refined perception and the direct experience of the divine can help put things in proportion but can also be hijacked to increase inflation. When we experience "I am God," it is important to be careful how far that is taken.

Adding to the issue can be a great increase in energy and sense of power. Ego can feed on that and try to regain control.

Unchecked, inflation can expand into a "Jesus Complex." This may lead someone to begin teaching but obviously not from an appropriate place. Yet they may gain adulation, which can be quite addictive and reinforce the delusion.

You can see why many traditional teachers offer everything they do to their teacher or the divine. They take no credit because they know it's not their doing.

In every case, where there is inflation there comes deflation. At some point, the claims will be seen through and collapse. This can be a difficult and humiliating experience, depending on how far we've bought into the story and how public it's been. Caplan's aforementioned book *Halfway Up The Mountain*[10] explores these issues in some detail. Ironically, one of her primary contributors fell into this himself.

Doubt

Inversely, when the mind tries to grasp the shift, it will find nothing to hold on to. There may be experiences and release that accompany the shift, but the shift itself is in being. It's the Self beyond the mind that awakens to Itself. The mind does not know or experience this.

This may not make sense to the mind. It can be fearful of a loss of control. So the mind may discount and doubt.

It can be very useful to have the support of a teacher in this period. Otherwise, there is the tendency to fall back into the mind and its old stories, especially if the shift was more delicate. If there has been a deep enough shift, clarity will return but it can take longer and be more difficult if we let the mind try to control it.

Doership

A key aspect of Self Realization is becoming an observer of the body-mind acting in the world. Where before we saw ourselves as the doer, making choices and in control, we've recognized now that this was an ego illusion. Ego was claiming doership of what was already happening without it. If witnessing came before Self Realization, we'll have experienced this prior.

Now we observe the mind thinking, the emotions arising, and the body acting, all with little or no apparent input from ourselves. We are no longer the doer, the actor on the stage of life. Yet life continues very much as it did before, and we continue to act to sustain our life.

The distinctiveness of this experience will depend on how strong the sense of separate witness is. If we feel more separateness, there will be a stronger sense of detachment from doing.

> But the man whose delight is in the Self alone, who is content in the Self, who rejoices only in the Self, for him there is no action that he need do.
>
> Neither has he any profit to gain in this life from the actions he has done or the actions he has not done; nor is

there any living creature on whom he need rely for any purpose.

Therefore, remaining unattached, always do the action worthy of performance. Engaging in action truly unattached, man attains to the Supreme.
— Krishna in the Bhagavad Gita[11]

If there is some understanding of this process or some refined perception has already developed, we may already recognize that action arises from the interplay of the laws of nature, both within us and around us. We may also inquire into this more closely, encouraging further refinement that we'll go into in the next stage.

The Resolute Intellect

Prior to Self Realization, the intellect is associated with mind and ego. It discriminates self and other as a protective response. It goes by the whims of the mind and is often driven by fear and the need to be right. It is biased by the mind's stories about the world.

As Self Realization becomes integrated, the intellect becomes associated with the stable, eternal Self instead. We see through some of our habitual stories and other filters and begin to see the world as it is more reliably. The intellect becomes resolute or clear and stable.

As this matures and perception refines, an ability known as "ritam" arises. When we are able to maintain attention on the level where the universe is first becoming, we can learn about the nature of whatever the attention is on or whatever arises in experience. This leads to the "inner guru" mentioned in Unity, as well as the ability to cognize, discussed further along.

> *Ritambharaa tatra pragjnaa, the intellect that knows only truth.*
> — Yoga Sutra 1.48[12]

If we're more oriented to intuition, this gains the same benefit. This becomes more significant further along.

Ananda or Bliss

As Self Realization matures, an ever-present inner happiness arises. The bliss body (kosha) becomes unhindered by the fading resistance of the mind and emotions. The Vedas call this maturation Sat Chit Ananda (absolute bliss consciousness). It is the Buddhist Nirvana.

The subjective presence of bliss will vary as life does: sometimes in the foreground, sometimes in the background. But it becomes largely ever-present, much as consciousness is beneath it. We come to know the very life that flows through our body as bliss.

> *He who knows this enjoyer of delight – the Self, the living soul, always near, lord of what was and what will be – no longer hides in fear.*
> — Katha Upanishad 2.1.5

For some, the bliss may come on during the initial honeymoon, then fade somewhat during the unloading process. But over time, it will become more established.

Like the awakening process though, bliss coming on-line is not a one-shot thing. Rather, it steps up progressively over time. The *Taittiriya Upanishad* (2.8) describes 10 stages, each 100 times the prior. In other words, it suggests an exponential scale. A new opening to bliss may rise gradually or come on quite intensely and unexpectedly as a rapture. If it kicks in suddenly, it can be almost overwhelming, leaving us crying with laughter. As several friends have joked, you hope this doesn't happen in public.

I've had a few such sudden upgrades. In one example, I wrote[13]: "I was driving down a main road in my truck. Suddenly a wave of happiness washed over me with such intensity that I was laughing out loud and crying at the same time. The sun burst through the clouds and bathed the truck in warmth and the radio played a song about being so "f***ing happy I could cry." Fortunately, the body took care of driving in traffic."

Tom Traynor mentions a public example in his *Buddha at the Gas Pump* interview[14]. Surprisingly quickly, we adapt to this new level of intense happiness, and it becomes the new norm. Happiness beyond conception becomes normal. That is, until it steps up again.

Duality

A big confusion in modern spiritual circles is around the term non-duality. In Self Realization, we are a distinct witness to a separate, possibly illusory, external world. There is inner silent Being observing separate outward change. This distinction between the observer and the world is known as dvaita (duality). Self Realization, as described here, is not advaita (non-duality). There may well be an inner sense of oneness but as long as there is separation, even from illusion, that is not it. As we will shortly see, actual non-duality comes further along.

Summary

The key shift here is from a sense of individual person to boundless being, a liberation. We become the detached observer or witness of our life (if not already). There is also commonly a deep inner peace and settledness as we step out of mind-identification. And there is often some back and forth involved in clearing and integrating the shift. As the process matures, an abiding happiness arises. The subjective experience and language used can differ widely.

Example Descriptions

[this person had witnessed for many years prior] On the day of my first shift at a satsang…, the silence in the environment and the inner witness became one. It was a very visceral experience for me.

When that happened there was an incredible release to freedom and unboundedness. I laughed, I cried and had hot flashes for many minutes, maybe 30 or more. When this subsided, I felt an incredible sense of peace and unboundedness. The unbounded witness/silence watched over everything I did. My awakening seemed to progress over a period of time. When I was involved in activity, I would initially lose the silent pure Awareness, but I could come back to it at any time.

After some time with the experience being the witness became truly unbounded. There was no beginning or

end to it and it was always there. I found that I could not locate my sense of who I was. Everything was still there but I did not relate to these outer things as who I was. There was no individual sense of self.
— anonymous[15]

There was an instantaneous change – from residing inside the body experiencing chaotic feelings and thoughts, to a view where I was not only behind that body but in a "place" where I was everywhere in my surroundings. The body was included in this place but "I" was not contained by it. Everything in this field of awareness was incredibly expanded. It was warmly brilliant and so very familiar. Flowing movement was one of the dominant characteristics along with the sense of freedom, well-being and joy.
— anonymous[16]

I can say that the initial stopping of the mind with eyes open, was a surprise. Not that it was unfamiliar, as a meditator for nearly 30 years, at the time, I had similar experiences eyes closed, but I guess I basically thought, mistakenly, that such depth and breadth of silence was only available with eyes closed. It was also a surprise that it really is that simple, and knowing that with the mind still, the mind itself could never "get" it. Once this great simplicity was available to me, there was a relaxation from "values," strains and struggles I previously held with such importance... now just a relaxation from such grips! And more simple surprises too.
— anonymous[17]

More often in activity, I am aware of a silent aspect of my Self which seems to be unaffected by the change and challenges of daily life. This part of me, when I recog-

nize it, seems to fill me with thrills of happiness that
lend a kind of non-attached perspective to my activity.
[This would be an example of a gradual or softer shift.]
— anonymous[18]

For the author, I was listening to a conference call satsang. Lorne Hoff used the word "surrender" for the first time[19], and I heard the word very differently than I ever had before. Something within let go and it was as if I fell into a transparent funnel. There was a relaxing and an opening and the perspective changed very distinctly.

At first I was uncertain what had happened. It was profound and dominant but subtle. Something had changed but what was it? No concepts could meet it. All ideas about it failed. Waking in the morning a day and a half later, a clarity and certainty had come. The shift was later verified.

The Next Transition

Some suggest awakening is the end of identification, but as we've seen, it is often just an upgraded version of winding things down. As we'll see further along, the ego has layers and there is more to resolve. Often, deeper layers fall away in later stages.

While Self Realization is a very profound and key shift, it is not full enlightenment. There can certainly be a distinctive sense of being done or complete. The seeker has fallen away and we're liberated. Life is bliss. There are ample teachers out there who will tell you, "This is it." But in many ways, it is only kindergarten. We have begun a remarkable post-personal journey into source.

How the next stage unfolds depends on the particular process. If there is sufficient sattva developed, there would typically be a God Consciousness phase next. If the process is more Atman-driven, the God Consciousness phase may not arise until later, if at all. In that case, the next clear shift happens at Unity, further along.

The speed of this process also varies widely. I've seen people take many years for the first shift to become reasonably clear. And I've seen people wake up and then have the Unity shift a few days later. There can also be blended variations. For example, Adyashanti had Unity elements in his initial awakening which then settled out. His actual Unity shift came several years later.

Notes

1 Dec. 21, 2007 letter

2 See his book *The End of Your World* in the Bibliography

3 eckharttolle.com

4 byronkatie.com

5 en.wikipedia.org/wiki/Eckhart_Tolle

6 See *The End Of Your World* in the Bibliography

7 With Adyashanti on the DVD *Journey after Awakening*

8 Satsang, July 2007, Vancouver

9 *The End of Your World*, Chapter 5

10 See Bibliography

11 *Bhagavad Gita* Ch 3, v17-19, translation by Maharishi Mahesh Yogi

12 Egenes translation

13 davidya.ca/2008/09/02/the-raptures/

14 batgap.com/tom-traynor

15 G.T.: lucialorn.net/#!cosmic-consciousness/c1m9w

16 L.C.: lucialorn.net/#!cosmic-consciousness3/c1pxe

17 M.S.: lucialorn.net/#!cosmic-consciousness-5/cxoo

18 The Supreme Awakening p183

19 2007-07-04 call, recording named *Silence Speaking to its Self*

Stage 1a
God Consciousness

I hear beyond the range of sound,
I see beyond the range of sight,
New earths and skies and seas around,
And in my day the sun doth pale in his light.
— Henry David Thoreau, *Inspiration*

This stage is also known as Refined Cosmic Consciousness or by some euphemisms like Divine or Celestial Consciousness to avoid the God word. But when refined perception of the world unfolds, divine intelligence and doership gradually become unmistakable. This doesn't mean we meet some big guy in a chair in the clouds or other religious icon. It means the divine play that underlies the world becomes obvious, and we recognize we're surrounded and supported by profound intelligence. As we go deeper into it, the layers of creation unfold to us and eventually, the source itself.

At the same time, this stage is a flowering of the heart and fine feelings. This may lead to a devotional phase, even in those not inclined to that. I'll come back to this shortly.

It's important to note here that this is not about belief. It doesn't matter if you're a theist, agnostic, or atheist. This is gnosis, direct experience. When it's clear, it is unmistakable. We may not use the God word, but we'll certainly come to know the divine.

How this experience unfolds varies immensely. Some people will awaken already conscious of subtler levels of existence. Because they're now immersed in it, the pace of that development can ramp up. Inversely, some will awaken with little awareness of anything non-physical. In that case, this stage may come as a surprise or may not show up until much later. I've seen people unfold God Consciousness in Brahman stage.

As with the other refined stages to follow, this stage is more about the clarity of perception and the awakening heart than Being or consciousness.

Perception

Your dominant sense and the perceptual channels that are clear will have a large impact on how this stage shows up. For some, this will be very visual. For others, more sound and vibration, and still others it will be through the body and sensation. As our connection deepens these perceptions will come with intelligence, with an understanding of what is being perceived. As I am a visual person, I naturally use visual words in my descriptions. But this is not a limitation on how it may unfold for you.

> *The hidden well-spring of your soul must needs rise and run murmuring to the sea; And the treasure of your infinite depths would be revealed to your eyes.*
> — Kahlil Gibran, *The Prophet*

Lorne Hoff observed that the refinement of perception may follow the mechanics of perception itself or the mechanics of consciousness, depending on your orientation[1]. This will shift what becomes known somewhat.

One of the key drivers of our process can be recognitions that arose during the prior stage. In Self Realization, we are a detached observer of our life as it unfolds before us, acting in the world.

We might then ask – who or what is doing the doing that continues after we stopped claiming it as ours? Choices are still being made. We might decide that these are residual habits of the personality, and to some extent this is true. But this doesn't address it all.

What we learn about are the laws of nature, the intelligence and principles that show up as thoughts and behaviour in our life. Some of those laws of nature will show up as routine functioning, some as talents and gifts, and some as less desirable tendencies. We didn't want to eat a donut, but there we are eating it. Each of us is a unique combination of the emphasis of various laws of nature.

Modes of Perception

Understanding how we recognize these laws requires

we unpack what I call modes of perception. There are two primary modes for relating to the world. We might call them intellect and heart, but it's more informative to say the Impersonal and the Personal. This distinction becomes much more obvious with the divine.

The Impersonal is the approach of the scientist and is dominant in the West. In this mode, the mind and intellect shift to recognizing the hand of the divine in the laws of nature and the profound intelligence that underlies all of creation. We recognize the principles and functions and their deeper origins.

In the Personal, we see those same principles personified based on our own expectations, culture, and how they choose to appear to us. In other words, we see beings of light of various types: nature's elementals; plant devas; beings with organizational responsibilities; divine beings. This is the mode of the open heart.

In either case, if this process goes deep enough, we will come to experience God in form. In fact, we may come to experience God in various forms, each exemplifying fundamental principles.

Yet one particular form will have profound personal relevance. We will relate to the divine most completely through our highest ideal in the form of our "Personal God." The form that takes cannot be guessed as it comes partly from their side and partly through the lens of our own expectations and ideals. The personal God will be a much deeper relationship than anything we've known prior.

Suffice to say, the divine will show up in ways unexpected as the dynamics of life unfold to us. The world's traditions are full of beautiful descriptions of the personal God, each unique to that person in that culture. One divine source can be known in as many ways as there are people.

Our own inclinations will determine the mode we favour, but both are available to us and have their advantages and disadvantages. The first is more objective and straightforward, good for the intellect. The second is richer and fuller, bringing a different type of knowledge. What better way to understand a law of nature than conversing with it? But ongoing, the personal can be too much information. It's easier to live day-to-day life in the impersonal, as most people do. We're here to live our physical lives for the most part. We can shift into the personal mode when required, much like shifting focus.

What is revealed to us and how we work with it varies widely. Perhaps we observe the flows of energy in a tree as it prepares for winter. Or we observe the plant devas, preparing their plants for the arrival of spring. Perhaps we're traveling by plane and the wind is rough. We can request that they move off a little to stop the turbulence. A friend had a large flock of birds move into his backyard and stay, beginning to do damage. He spoke with the bird devas and they moved. The possibilities are extensive.

This process allows us to discover a far greater range of life than we ever thought possible. We are never, ever alone. Even our body is packed with life forms, taking care of the minutiae of our well-being. Science already knows this, but only on the physical level.

Those principles of existence that science studies can be experienced directly for ourselves, at all scales. This means that some things commonly considered meta-physical or delusional may become a normal part of our day-to-day life. Light beings, how the world comes into form, auras, the flow of the divine, and so forth can become part of our normal experience. Many of those big questions about life, the universe, and every-thing are resolved.

At first, the koshas (sheaths) are recognized as distinct layers, even like distinct worlds. But in actuality, it is all in the same space at different resolutions. As our perception refines, those finer resolutions become ap-parent. Then these "worlds" come to be recognized in a larger context, more like a rainbow of inter-penetrat-ing values.

We may come to perceive the flow of life in all life forms, like the shift of seasons mentioned above. Or we may come to see the bliss body (anandamaya) as golden light radiating from people's heads like a halo or see all life or the world immersed in it. There are many, many potential layers and experiences here.

What we are experiencing are the finer values of Con-sciousness in its own becoming. Old concepts and boundaries fall away from both the lived boundless-ness and the changed perception of the world. Same world, much deeper and fuller experience.

The Heart

This stage is also characterized by the awakening of the heart on a much deeper level. This is not the initial heart awakening (anahata chakra) that may be noticed during the rise of kundalini Shakti. Rather it is a much deeper value of divine heart (hridaya) during the post-awakening descent. This opening triggers an outflowing of universal love and may well be accompanied by a devotional phase, even in those whose intellect is dominant.

> *Bring yourself to the source of Love and you have all love, universal love.*
> — Maharishi Mahesh Yogi, *Love and God*

Because of the profound outpouring of love, we may seek an object of devotion. The Vedic texts suggest we may choose our favoured form of God, our teacher, or our upaguru as our object of devotion. Upaguru is our mate or loved one, raised in perception to their divinity. This is "Namaste" lived as reality. It is not a mood or emotion, it is a vast open space in the chest lit up and pouring forth at the limits of our capacity. It is the divine itself, flowing out through us.

This heart opening dissolves the energetic drivers (emotions) of the old ego-concept. Without emotional energy, those aspects of the mind still trying to control will shrivel and fade away.

It also lets us recognize the flow of love that is ever-present, underlying all experience and form. This brings a massive influx of fine and profound feelings, often well beyond anything in prior experience. It is a profundity of heart that we could not have conceived of.

Soon, the divine aspect of our own apparently individual feelings, mind, body, and so forth becomes increasingly obvious. The divine is flowing through us. We are of it and never apart.

This can profoundly trump Self Realization. Maharishi Mahesh Yogi described this as the two fullnesses – fullness within and fullness of the world.

Soma

While cleansing the windows of perception is key, they must also be refined to perceive finer values. The mechanism of refinement of perception and the physiology is a pre-physical substance called soma. Soma is a refined product of the body produced in samadhi. Like samadhi, it is transitory at first but becomes ongoing.

In the center of the brain, we have a connection to a raw form of soma that surrounds us. When we touch source, soma enters there and filters down through the brain, dripping out of a subtle organ in the back of the throat. There it mixes with saliva and we may notice a sweet taste. We then swallow it down into digestion.

From the digestive system, the devas (laws of nature) are fed and enriched. Combine that with the upgrade from suffering to bliss, and we create a much nicer energetic environment for our energy beings. Keep in mind that such beings live in the world of energy and feeling so we're giving them a quality of life upgrade. Sometimes it is a pretty major one.

With awakening, we shift from samadhi in meditation to being in a form of samadhi all the time. If we get enough sleep and take decent care of it, the body can ramp up soma production. Refinement feeds further refinement.

As we've now become a better "employer," this also attracts new laws of nature that were not available to us prior. The result is much enhanced support, opportunities, and abilities. Even when there is difficult karma (energy) arising, it can more smoothly move through our lives.

The Ninth Mandala of the Rig Veda talks extensively about flowing soma through the "filter." While there are ceremonial representations of this, you are the filter being described.

At a deep level, we are immersed in that sea of milk from which the cosmic body arises. When our body is sufficiently purified, it becomes a manufacturing center for soma in the body.

This process of soma may at first be known only by its effects, like much easier results in the world or finer perception. Then it might be tasted in the throat. Eventually we come to witness parts of this process directly. And then we become the flow itself. We are the soma, nourishing the devas of the cosmic body, the body of all bodies of all beings in this creation. I'll come back to this subject later on, but this perhaps gives you an idea of why very enlightened beings are so precious. They support us on a scale we cannot even comprehend.

Soma Is Not

It should be emphasized that these are not philosophical or religious concepts I describe but things that can be directly experienced as aspects of your own nature. We are the "son" of God and return home through our recognition of our cosmic, then divine nature.

While other things may have such a name, this soma is not a plant nor is it a hallucinogenic mushroom. Subtle perception is nothing like the distortion of a drug trip. The Vedas are not mythical texts but do arise from a distinct culture with its own perspectives from long ago in a different age.

Gifts and Abilities

Because we're opening up new energy channels and refining the energy physiology, there is a tendency for gifts we have to become activated or to become much clearer and stronger. It is also possible for new abilities to be enabled. The nature of these gifts varies widely and may be either unique or a more common potential. It depends on the need of the person and the time.

The third book of the Yoga Sutra of Patanjali describes dozens of common ones. The text describes using the technique of Samyama (open awareness focused on a specific intention) for a specific effect. But such abilities arise spontaneously as well. Some examples from the text include knowledge of past lives, understanding the vocalizations of all living beings, knowledge of death, effulgence, friendliness, great strength, and so forth. It also includes seemingly impossible things like being able to fly or turn invisible. In all cases, the text tells how. But the full expression requires a physiology clear enough for the intention to flow unimpeded.

If you think flying, for example, is ludicrous, there are a number of well-documented historical cases like Milarepa, Hu San Gong, and St. Joseph of Cupertino[2]. It was also practiced in some aboriginal cultures.

However, a lot of this type of development is ignored, dismissed, or skimmed over by the strong minds of Westerners. We're more individualistic and less emotionally open with more carefully guarded hearts. Thus, fewer Westerners are experiencing the refined values early on. Some don't go through a God Consciousness phase, just Self Realization and maybe Unity. But without this development, the fullness and richness of enlightenment will not unfold.

Summary

This stage, God Consciousness, is part of a process that can begin long before the first stage or well after. It also continues through and past all stages of development in consciousness. However, this actual stage doesn't begin until Self Realization is established and Shiva-Shakti descends to the heart, awakening its divine values. As Maharishi Mahesh Yogi said[3], we cannot realize God until we have realized the Self.

This stage has two aspects: the divine heart opening and the refinement of perception. The first wakes us to values of love and divine presence the mind could not have conceived of. The second is a gradual shift into recognizing the world as a divine play. As described in the Gunas above, this requires sufficient sattva for the clarity to move beyond world-as-illusion.

Example Descriptions

For instance, when looking at a tree, I first become aware of the object as it is – a concrete form bound in space and time. But then I perceive finer aspects of the object coexisting along with its concrete expression. On this subtler level, objects are perceived as almost transparent structures of soft, satiny light (unlike harsher, normal daylight) through which the very essence of life appears to flow. This flowing field of life underlies and permeates the objects of perception. Perceiving these finer aspects of creation completely nourishes the finest aspect of my own being.
— anonymous[4]

There were days when I felt my heart melting, as if I could take everything in creation into myself and cherish it with the greatest love. Often I would have long periods of the day when everything I saw seemed to be glowing with divine radiance. Sometimes I would even be able to see the tremendous energy at the basis of every object, minute particles of energy (light?) moving very rapidly at a different rate and pattern for every object, yet unified somehow...
— anonymous[5]

The silent ocean of pure love draws my awareness inward and bathes my heart in a sweet nectar-like fullness that cannot be described, and yet I feel that this sweetness is unlimited in its exquisite magnitude. There is so much more to be experienced. I feel that the power of the Self and the power of God are being revealed at the same time.[notice the distinction/separation here] I am finding that love, which I have sought all my life, exists within my Self – within the very heart of creation,

within the temple of the heart, at the feet of God.
— anonymous[6]

For the author, there was a breaking open of the heart as the energy of awakening descended there. Love overflowed. When love rose in the physiology, it expressed as compassion. When it descended, passion flowered. I entered a devotional phase and there came a profound need to direct the overflowing love to those around me. It could not be contained. At a satsang, some of those around me were overwhelmed with happiness. One woman even fainted from joy, falling out of her chair onto my back. I saw the world as created in every moment, immersed in a golden ocean of light. Life was everywhere, in everything. All the past and future collapsed into the present moment, existing simultaneously and concurrently.

Fortunately, this became better integrated and I stopped disorienting other people as much.

"The ebb and flow of bliss as it ripples through Itself, shifting, then exploding in expression and love," I wrote then.

The Next Transition

This phase of refinement cannot flower fully until after established Unity that follows. The context is not yet complete.

The transition to Unity is classically described as the progressive refinement of perception until we recognize ourselves under the finest value of the relative world. However, this would require good sattva development which may not be present yet. Key is that consciousness becomes so deeply established within itself that it recognizes itself in the world.

Notes

1 Retreat in September 2015
2 See Pearson's book *The Complete Book of Yogic Flying*
3 *Gaining UC* talk, Amherst, June, 1971
4 The Supreme Awakening p268
5 The Supreme Awakening p267
6 The Supreme Awakening p270

Stage 2
Unity Consciousness

He who sees everything as nothing but the Self,
and the Self in everything he sees,
such a seer withdraws from nothing.
For the enlightened, all that is is nothing but the Self,
so how could any suffering or delusion continue
for those who know this oneness?
— Isha Upanishad v6-7

As we deepen into the day-to-day experience of awakened life, at some point the subject or observer is discovered to be underlying everything around us. We may come to this through refined perception, bliss, or the intensity of consciousness itself. When the same Self is recognized right in the objects of experience of the world, right on the surface of life, the Unity shift occurs. We shift from being the observer of all life to being all life and all existence. We can say the observer and object sides of consciousness merge when recognized as the same Self.

For some, Unity begins with a single distinct shift. For others, there can be a few brief steps in the approach, such as the resolution of the core identity (below), a recognition that we contain the world or there is no longer a separation, and then the Unity realization itself.

While the God Consciousness phase is dominated by the heart, the Unity shift is one for the intellect. It is the intellect that makes the recognition and continues the process. Previously the intellect saw distinctions and divided this from that. With the recognition of underlying oneness, it sees oneness in every experience and joins that to the whole. That is the Self, and that, and that… Recall that the intellect is now "resolute," led by Self rather than ego.

Core Identity

The gut holds a sub-conscious sense of core identity. This is an energetic resistance that is driven by an until-now deeply sub-conscious fear response to the ancient experience of being separated from the divine. We may not call the emotion we discover here "fear" but it will be related. It's like a core grasping at something to hold on to in our alone separateness.

Because of the 3-layer nature of the ego: mental concept (resolved in 1), emotional drivers (1a) and core identity (2), I jokingly called them the 3 Am-Egos. This is the last of the head, heart, gut descent described earlier.

Because this is the origin of our sense of separate identity, it has an association with our name. It is the core I Am. I've seen energy workers describe the effects of our core identity as the Protectors that defend our energetic presence. It can be heavily fortified. When it releases, we may find our name no longer suits for a time. There is also an end of the separation between the sense of inside and outside.

Adyashanti and Loch Kelly described[1] a "barbecue" that happens with this release in their *Journey After Awakening* talk. When the core identity or separation in the gut is finally seen, the release may be experienced like a barbecue or roasting. Some will notice a very distinct or even prolonged barbecue; Adyashanti described his taking two weeks to resolve. Others may not notice this step or perhaps notice just a brief, distinctive release. The gut release may also be experienced as another rise in those with more of a Shakti orientation.

For a while I thought this was a key feature of the Unity shift even if it was quite mild or brief for some. But since then, I've seen examples where this core fear is not resolved until later. Susanne Marie, for example, described the "existential identity" releasing at the end of Unity instead[2]. I've also seen someone have the heart opening (1a) post-Brahman, meaning the gut release is yet to come.

Until this last core fear is resolved, there is still a subconscious desire for protection and control that can re-identify or revive. (see the Inflation section prior) Once it is cleared, that tendency to a "spiritualized ego" should finally end.

However, we may still have deep unresolved nuts that can compromise clarity. Over time in Unity, remaining subtle "shoulds" and "musts" fall away, liberating this expression. These are somewhat like the shrapnel cleared after the first shift but more subtle. Less like stories, they're experienced more like pre-conscious urges with a quality of resistance and defense.

Curiously, this clearing can lead to the person becoming more distinct as the old constraints fall away. This has been true of many of history's famous saints and sages.

Even with this release, there are still habits of being that express as preferences and inclinations. A "person" or human continues, but now as a part of this expression rather than as who I am. We might call the person a cluster of laws of nature. More like our thumb, it is a useful tool but not a limitation on who we are.

Perception

In Unity, there are still perceived forms with boundaries. But those boundaries only exist in the senses. We know directly that those boundaries are just an appearance. The world is now progressively seen as consciousness in the guise of the mind, body, and world. Assuming there is sufficient refinement of perception, we come to directly experience the flow of consciousness within all form. The world is known as flowing attention and intention, as consciousness itself.

The sense of illusory world has flipped again and we find what was real within is also present right in the world. This is not the same real we experienced prior to awakening to the Self but rather a greater, more concrete reality. Form is recognized as nothing but eternal infinite consciousness. This gives it a profound solidity. Not an objective physical reality but one of pure subjectivity. All is my Self, very literally.

Perception also takes on a profound intimacy as discussed in Placement of Attention shortly.

What is United?

In Self Realization, there is a distinct difference between the inner silent observer and the outer liveliness (change) of creation. After Unity, the subject and object become one, leaving only experiences taking place within that container of self-aware consciousness.

But as the subject and object (masculine and feminine) are merged, so are silence and liveliness. Absolute silence is no more. Consciousness is lit.

> *When you make the two one, and you make the inside as the outside and the outside as the inside and the above as the below, and if you establish the male with the female as a single unity... then shall you enter the Sovereignty (kingdom).*
> — Jesus, Gospel of Thomas

It's Progressive

Long habits of seeing objects as separate means that we need time to experience them as my Self. We progressively experience and become whatever arises. This is the key process of Unity; a progressive uniting through experiencing life. All the layers of experience and memory are united into one wholeness.

Combine the Resolute Intellect mentioned previously with this process of becoming, and we gain knowing by being. Whatever we put our attention on, we become or recognize we've always been. If there is enough clarity in that channel of experience, the inherent intelligence in the object of perception is revealed and can flow. We know it because we are it. Some call this the "inner guru."

> *By virtue of unitedness and by means of that which remains to be united, I perform action to generate wholeness of life.*
> — Rig Veda[3]

The Brahma Sutra, core text of Vedanta (meaning "end of the Veda"), is said to be a list of realizations of this process. Every translation I've seen has mistakenly seen the text as philosophical arguments. Shankara's commentary on the text certainly is, but not the text itself. Each sutra (thread) is a recognition of the intellect that not only brings together more and more of the field of experience into an "aggregate" or wholeness but also thins the remaining ignorance. Again, we know it because we become it.

It is a process of simply living life while direct experience draws more and more together. This goes on to include the farthest ranges of consciousness, beyond sensory experience. We are it so we can know it.

> *Even the farthest reaches of the galactic universe which we can't see are still concretely cognized and appreciated as an expression of the Self.*
> — Maharishi Mahesh Yogi[4]

Stages of Unity

Maharishi Mahesh Yogi described Unity as taking place in 10 stages, corresponding to the 10 mandalas (books) of the Rig Veda. He described this in two ways; by the prakriti (nature) being unified and by the subjective experience[5].

10 Stages of Unity
1) Atman: stirring aliveness, the liveliness of silence
2) Earth: deeper, aliveness seen in objects
3) Water: observer moving into the flow
4) Fire: witness engages in perception
5) Air: deepening on level of energy
6) Space: space seen on surface
7) Mind: cosmic mind
8) Intellect: cosmic intellect
9) Ego: cosmic intelligence, mechanics of soma
10) Brahman: Purusha, Brahman stage

> *The smriti (cosmic memory) of wholeness is recalled when the intellect recognizes itself as intelligence.*
> — Maharishi Mahesh Yogi

I didn't find the process this tidy, but the values showed up in various ways. This also offers insight into the organization of the Rig Veda. Notice how there is an inner progression very similar to childhood development discussed back at the beginning: world, mind, intellect, ego.

Inversely, there is also embodiment. In the embodiment process, the cosmic is moving forward from within. First, we discover we are Cosmic Self in Self Realization. Then there is a progressive recognition of the cosmic in all layers of being until we recognize that even the physical body is cosmic and always was. We are the one body experiencing itself through many forms. I explore this more in Refined Unity shortly.

This perhaps makes it clear that non-duality typically arises as a process. Unity is a progression of uniting that climaxes with Brahman, resolving even subtle dualities.

Placement of Attention

As we become it, everything takes on a much greater intimacy. When the process moves into the senses, we touch an object and we feel the object. But as we also are the object, literally, we also feel being touched at the same time. We are everything we put our attention on.

Because we are it, this also means we can easily perceive through whatever we have the attention on. We can experience what it is to be a tree or cat or another person. However, we are experiencing through our value of consciousness not theirs, so our experience is not exactly the same as that being's. We experience their experience through their senses, but with "our eyes" so to speak. Recall what it was like to be 8 years old. We remember it from where we are now, not from how we were then.

In other words, we can get a real sense of what it's like to be another being but not exactly how they are experiencing it. Also, just as we can know our own past incarnations, we progressively find ourselves aware of all beings and their entire history as well. Even time is merged into one wholeness.

We can also experience what it is to be the wind, a rock, a community, or any other thing we can experience. We are it so it is only a matter of placement of attention.

> *You are woman. You are man. You are the youth and the maiden too. You are the old man hobbling along with a staff. Once born, you are the face turned in every direction.*

> *You are the dark blue butterfly, you are the green parrot with red eyes. You are the thundercloud, pregnant with lightning. You are the seasons, you are the seas. You are without beginning, present everywhere. You, from whom all worlds are born.*
> — Shvetaashvatara Upanishad 4.3-4

Of course, such experience is limited by how clear our various channels are. Plus, different people will have different interests that unfold different aspects of the vastness of creation. Some will have no interest in the past, for example, but may be very interested in the structure of matter. That will lead to some expertise in one but not the other.

The Remains

There is also a key idea for Unity known as Lesha Avidya (pronunced leishavidya), the faint remains of ignorance. A traditional analogy is that after you put down a ball of butter, there is still a film of butter on your hands. It doesn't impede your hands touching other things but a small shadow remains. We continue to be human. We continue to have blind spots and gaps. We can continue to learn and grow.

Lesha Avidya can also refer to keeping a small space between oneself and our object of devotion, a chosen small ignorance. This point is important in God Realization, which we'll explore coming up.

Summary

With the Unity shift, the Self that had been realized within is also realized to be in the world. Subject and object collapse together into simply experiencing. Silence has become lively. The Unity process takes place progressively through living life as we experience and recognize everything as ourselves. This deepens through memory in time and space until all is united.

Example Descriptions

The experience of being unbounded pure Consciousness was an absolutely clear and permanent reality, and I thought that there couldn't be anything more than being Consciousness itself, until one summer evening... "I" (Being) was seized by an intensely alive, unknown Wholeness which was so intense, so all encompassing that it seemed to be swallowing Being, as if "I" (Being) was dying.

Even though there was no self and no fear there was still a kind of trepidation. The thought came, "I am pure Being itself, how can pure Being be dying? Suddenly an inner/outer transformation occurred and "I" (Being) literally exploded and became that great Wholeness that was swallowing me. I became everything, everywhere in the environment, from the subtle to the gross – the

atoms, the air, the space, the light, the solid walls, the furniture, the hills, the trees, everything everywhere, was all One grand wholeness of Self.
— anonymous[6]

Everything was in me, I was everything and felt intimate with everything. I am the waves of joy and bliss. I see from here, there and everywhere. I am the seeing. Everything exists in my seeing. The subject and the object are contained in the seeing, there is no separation.

I am starting to become what I see. I am sadness, happiness, anger or joy in what ever is in my seeing. I sometimes feel the concepts of the people that I am seeing. (It is difficult to use words to describe my experience because the individual "I" does not exist even though the form that I was still exists. The individual form is part of the all that I am).
— anonymous[7]

As we sat in meditation I noticed the silence intensify and the stillness become more alive and vibrant. I also noticed a sense of my body mind dissolving and no finding of the body even though of course the physical body was still there. I looked at my body and I could see it and feel it but I also had this strange sense that it was not there but was now everywhere. It felt different from the expanded unboundedness I had been experiencing since the first shift.
— anonymous[8]

Being said, "oh, of course, I am all this too" and then the infinite Being that I thought I was shot out on to the surface of life like a water spout, and I became everything everywhere.

The change was instant and silent Being as witness disappeared. At first it was disconcerting because what had been the existence for 4 years was lost, but in time the new existence of being infinity as everything on the surface of life became comfortable and normal.
— anonymous[9]

The prevailing sense now is that I am the entire universe. I happen to see and speak from here, but that seems almost incidental, just a reference point for the sake of perception. When I look at anything, I see consciousness... I see subjectivity which has taken form, which has adopted an appearance of matter. I perceive the boundaries of the objective, material world, but I see them as boundaries on the surface of a more significant underlying reality – that consciousness, my own consciousness, comprises all that there is.
— anonymous[10]

For the author, the shift happened in several short steps. First there was a descent to the gut and a deeper level of I-sense discovered, a core fear that arose from an ancient separation from the divine in the cycles of time. Now conscious, it was quickly released. Loch Kelly described this as the barbeque, mentioned above. This was more distinct but subtler than losing the me-sense with the initial awakening. The sense of "David" that was tied to this core identity was now roasted. For a week or so, there was no sense of personal so I dropped personal pronouns entirely, referring to the body-mind as the "unit." Friends joked about the person "formerly known as David." In day-to-day experience it became clear there was no longer a separation between inside and outside. I contained the world.

A short time later, I went on a weekend retreat and there was an evening surrender. All prior experiences, all prior awakening, everything was released and vanished. What remained was wholeness. Gradually, what had been came back again but now in this very new context, including the person named David. Everything and everyone was within my Self and of my Self. This progressively deepened over time, partly through becoming (recognizing I was) everything that arose in experience, as described earlier.

The Next Transition

After the contrast of the shift into Unity, whatever refined qualities that had developed in the prior refined phase come back on-line in the new context. Unity may be a distinct shift with a loss of those refined values for a time, or the refined perception may simply carry forward into the new context. If the second is the case, Unity and Refined Unity won't be seen as distinct stages as much. However, the refinement now has a very new context and can grow in new directions.

Notes

1 DVD: *Journey After Awakening*
2 davidya.ca/2016/11/19/on-the-falling-away-of-self-adyashanti-and-susanne-marie/
3 Tenth mandala, 2nd to last verse
4 Paraphrasing the Vedas
5 Outlined by teachers to me on several occasions
6 L.W.: lucialorn.net/#!unity-consciousness/csk6
7 G.T.: lucialorn.net/#!unity-consciousness/csk6
8 C.B.: lucialorn.net/#!unity-consciousness/csk6

9 L.U.: lucialorn.net/#!unity-consciousness/csk6

10 Supreme Awakening p325

Stage 2a
Refined Unity Consciousness

Now comes the final merging,
Now comes everlasting beauty,
Now comes abundant grace,
now comes boundless purity.
— Rumi

This is further development of the prior refinement, but now in the new context of Unity, from the perspective of progressively being everything. Everything is in the devata value; everything is the process of experience as there is no longer a separate subject and object.

Just as we came to know the subtle and divine before, now it is experienced from the new perspective of oneness and being all that is. We come to recognize the flow of consciousness that underlies and creates all forms and phenomena and the layers of intelligence in the Self. This flow can dominate our sensory perceptions and be right on the surface; form can be like a ghost behind it or around it. Or flow can be like a "transparent sap" moving within form. This can also be simultaneous with other layers of subtle perception like energy or devata.

Consciousness becomes clearly aware of its own internal dynamics, how it creates and experiences. It awakens to its own intelligence that gives structure to the appearance of all that is: your life, the world, the universe, and all of its underpinnings. Consciousness is perceptually experienced as the ground of all that is.

> *It is Consciousness awakening to its own internal dynamics as the perpetual flow of itself knowing itself. It is the experience of the ultimate reality of the total depth of the Self, the totality of Consciousness, and it is all Divine.*
> — Lorne Hoff[1]

How that comes to be known subjectively will vary widely with each person. It may be seen, felt, heard, simply known, or some combination of these. If the refinement is well along, this will be a very full and rich experience.

However, even though the mechanics of consciousness have become intimate to us, the cause of awakening is still not seen. We may refer to it as grace, the hand of the divine.

Chhandas

Another dynamic that begins to gain significance is the dissolution of the second covering. Where in earlier refinement, we dissolved the veil of the world, now we begin to dissolve the veil of consciousness itself. If we use the analogy of a movie, before we were distracted by the images on the screen, the movie of the world. Then we became aware of the screen of consciousness behind it and saw the world as an appearance. Now we dissolve the second covering, the screen itself.

Self-aware consciousness can be said to have three aspects as mentioned earlier: observer, process of experience, and object of experience. In Sanskrit, these are known as rishi, devata, and chhandas. When the object value, chhandas, is seen as separate, it turns consciousness into an opaque container. This is the screen on which the appearance of the world plays. With Unity, objects are recognized as ourselves and are merged with the subject. We are one with the world.

However, some habits of relating to the world continue, so it takes some time for the opacity of the screen to dissolve. This becomes key for consciousness to be seen through and the next stage to unfold.

This process is also described as cutting the knots that bind us to consciousness.

The Cosmic: Part 1

As we touched on earlier, a related process is the progressive knowing and uniting with the cosmic (universal) structures of creation. There were references to the cosmic in the 10 Stages of Unity above: cosmic mind, cosmic intellect, and cosmic ego. We might call this the cosmic subject.

Becoming the Structure of Creation

A similar process in observing the structure of creation goes like this: I am the Universe (Aham Vishvam); I am the Devata (Devo Hum) who express all forms; I am the Cosmic Body (Aham Shrivir), the body of all bodies; I am the Veda (Veda Hum), the blueprint of creation.

First, we recognize ourselves bodily as the Universe. Our body is and contains the universe. Then, we discover the devata body that is full of "points of light" which manage the details of the appearance of all beings in all time concurrently. We experience our body as the devata body. And then we know our body as the cosmic body that is the body of all bodies. Finally, we know the body as Veda, the knowledge and blueprints that structure everything. We recognize ourselves as the one cosmic being in all layers of experience.

This also brings the cosmic subject and objects together experientially.

This process unfolds in the reverse order of its expression because we climb reality in our return home to source. Of course, there will be lots of variation in how this is experienced and described.

Also, there may be sub-stages of these realizations:
– recognition that there is a cosmic body
– recognition that I am that, becoming it experientially
– integration as a deeper becoming that is more embodied
– recognition that even the physical body is cosmic, the cosmic sense of person

– merging the physical, cosmic, and divine post-Brahman.

I'll come back to this topic in two more sections after the Brahman shift.

Cognition: Part 1

Not everyone has [the] ability to be a seer, to cognize, but everyone can realize.
— Maharishi Mahesh Yogi[2]

The full range of the koshas is available to everyone for progressive refinement and experience, but there is another distinct style of experience called cognition.

This is where the rishi comes in. Rishi is a Sanskrit word meaning seer. Rishi is sometimes equated with guru or teacher, but a seer is simply one who sees reality. They may not be a teacher. They also may not yet be awake as I've seen cognitions arise prior. But it would seem makara is required so there is a stable platform and the lights are on (the 6th chakra). More advanced tiers of cognition would require higher stages.

Three Tiers of Cognition.

1) Basic Cognition

This first level of cognition occurs when deep laws of nature that are lively in consciousness are experienced directly by the seer. In this form of experience, there is direct perception, but the perception is total: it comes with a perception of the object from all angles, from all time, and with complete understanding about it. The cognition itself takes a short time but once the door is open, it remains available to explore permanently. It can be a massive experience that takes months to unfold to the mind so it can be digested and explained.

For example, Hiranya Garbha, the golden egg or seed form of the universe, can be experienced as an object in one of the koshas, but it can also be cognized. When cognized, it includes the entirety of the universe, its history and progression, and how it operates. A cognition like this can take months to unpack.

There is a plethora of smaller realizations that may take less time. I suspect it would be typical for seers to begin at this tier.

2) Re-Cognition

This level of cognition occurs when laws of nature that have grown dormant are revived in consciousness, activating them in nature. It is a re-enlivenment in the current time, helping move things along that have gone stagnant in the cycles of time.

Once awake, these laws can intertwine with other awake laws, creating new synergies that further evolve life. I've noticed this going on in the current time as group consciousness progressively awakens.

From that reawakening, a larger number of seers can have a basic cognition of those same values, helping to enliven those principles further and get them more expressed. Specific people will embody specific combinations of laws in their expression of the cosmic body to support a unique synthesis that meets the need of the time.

Remember that this is an inside-out process. Awakening laws of nature deep within can take time to show up on the surface. Often, what we first see are disruptions when what hinders flow is pushed to the surface to be seen and cleared. This process is prominent in current world events and is sometimes not being well handled.

3) Vedic or Primary Cognition

Maharishi Mahesh Yogi said that this stage of cognition does not arise until after Brahman is established. We'll explain further in the Brahman stage, once the reader has the context for its unfolding.

Summary

The same process of the prior refinement continues, but now in this new context of Unity. Refined perception massively expands the fields of experience and thus the fields that are being united. The cosmic values of life become lived in the world.

Example Descriptions

> *I am the movement -- all of it, the ebb, the flow, the light, the dark, the oneness, the movement moving, the stillness alive with silent awareness, vibrantly breathing it all into being, the wholeness whole. I am so grateful for the beautiful unfolding of this process, so beautiful... intense at moments yes but so, so beautiful! Resting in the unknown and love so infinite...*
> — anonymous[3]

When walking outside I notice the scenery filled with some new quality, some vitality beyond description. I see both the unbounded and boundaries existing together, both the tree and the sky as one underlying wholeness, the finite and infinite blended together in one totality. It is indescribable to be seeing the same scenery in a different way, without having done anything. I see infinity expressed everywhere, and nowhere can I find the finite only.
— anonymous[4]

To see the Oneness of everything is like having special 3D glasses put before your eyes; I thought to myself: for sure, this is what they mean when they say "God IS everywhere."

I could have stood there looking for the rest of my life, but after awhile, I thought it was all too good to be true; it was some hoax of the mind and when the bell rang, it would all disappear. Well the bell finally rang, and it rang the next day and for the rest of the week, but the 3D glasses were still intact. What I had taken as a trick of the mind was to become a permanent way of seeing and knowing...
— Bernadette Roberts[5]

For the author, there were many layers of unfolding, but perhaps most significant was the intelligence within experiences revealing itself. This means that many experiences came with their own profound understanding. The universal dynamics of consciousness and the world were revealed. The unfolding described in the Cosmic section and the laws of nature in the Cognition section also unfolded.

The Next Transition

There are several aspects that may be involved in the approach to Brahman. Key is that as the unification reaches its completion, there are key climactic recognitions.

The Mahavakya

In the West, the most famous phrases from the Upanishads are I am That, Thou art That, all this is That, and That alone is. They are called the great sayings or mahavakya. It is said that they given by the teacher at the key moment of realization. But usually students already have them so the realization is unimpeded.

At one point, I also saw them as the recognition of each prior stage. However, "That" is a reference to Brahman which is not really part of the picture until the coming shift. Also, the above sequence turns out to be a Westernization.

They are more accurately framed as four ways the transition may be recognized subjectively. Note that a mahavakya is a recognition of the intellect which makes it late in the Unity process. The shift to Brahman goes beyond the intellect. Brahman is remembered.

1) **Prajnanam Brahma** – "Knowledge is Brahman" or "That alone Is"
(Aitareya Upanishad 3.3 of the Rig Veda)

2) **Ayam Atma Brahma** – "This Self (Atman) is Brahman" or "All This is That"
(Mandukya Upanishad 1.2 of the Atharva Veda)

3) **Tat Tvam Asi** – "Thou art That"
(Chandogya Upanishad 6.8.7 of the Sama Veda)

4) **Aham Brahmasmi** – "I am Brahman (That)"
(Brhadaranyaka Upanishad 1.4.10 of the Yajur Veda)

They were compiled by the sage Shankara. Note that each one comes from one of the 4 primary Vedas.

Other mahavakyas you may see include:
Ekam Evadvitiyam Brahma – "Brahman is one, without a second"
(Chandogya Upanishad 6.2.1 of the Sama Veda)

Sarvam Khalvidam Brahma – "All of this is Brahman"
(Chandogya Upanishad 3.14.1 of the Sama Veda)

A Climax of Refinement: God Realization

Where the stages in consciousness begin with a realization or becoming, the refined stages climax with a realization. If there has been a strong refinement stage underway, there will have been an unfolding relationship with the divine in some form, often in appearance as a "Personal God." Through the process of uniting, we are led to the climax of becoming called God Realization. With the fullness of the expressed divine in direct experience, we unite with the divine. However, this comes with a choice. We may unite with God fully or retain a small separation so we can remain close to God in relationship. This is a choice between you and the divine that will happen when the time comes.

We can describe this choice as between the Personal and the Impersonal:

112

1) Personal

In the personal we choose to remain in relationship with the divine, so we retain a small gap or separation to keep the flow of love and devotion going. By virtue of Lesha Avidya, a faint remains of ignorance (described in Unity above), we continue to play with God.

2) Impersonal

The impersonal route means uniting in complete Oneness with God. We surrender even our deep relationship with God. Expressed divine and the cosmic Self are recognized as one.

The people I've discussed this with all chose the second route or don't relate to it this way. If they do relate, oneness with God became the doorway into Brahman. It was the last thing to Unite.

The Approach

By this point, we have deepened into the entire breadth of Self and have come to recognize that Self is ever awake and globally aware. In addition, it is aware of itself at every point within that global awareness. Some of those points are experiencing through an apparent form as a being and other points know themselves as objects. There are of course various ways this may be recognized and described. The key is the recognition of both global and at-every-point. This is complete wholeness.

We have now come to know the totality of consciousness. The "aggregate" or wholeness described in the Brahma Sutra is complete. There are no longer any stages of development in consciousness possible.

At this point, the covering value of consciousness (chhandas above) dissolves enough that we see through it. An unexpected thing then happens. Fully aware of its own Self, Self stops looking perpetually in on itself and turns to look beyond itself.

There, to its surprise, Atman discovers its own origins. Before, we saw Atman as infinite and eternal. Now we recognize there is something beyond Atman and that eternal, infinite Being has an origin, although not in the sense of time.

There can be several kinds of recognition in this process. There may be a mahavakya, like this Self is Brahman! Or if there has been a major sattva process, some form of God Realization will transpire.

Through some form of recognition, we transcend consciousness, existence, and Atman into Brahman. We shift from alive everything into absolute nothingness (not to be confused with emptiness). Brahman is remembered.

Notes

1 lucialorn.net/states-of-consciousness

2 Recording: *Mechanics of Perception of Man in BC and Vedic Seer*, May 26, 1975

3 C.B.: lucialorn.net/#!more-ucshift/c1gd3

4 Supreme Awakening p327

5 *The Experience of No-Self*

Stage 3
Beyond Consciousness

Using the nature of his own Self (Atman),
like a lamp to illumine the true nature of Brahman.
— Shvetaashvatara Upanishad 2.15

The Vedas call this the Great Awakening. Brahman means "the great" and is prior to consciousness, prior to intelligence, and prior to existence itself. It is neither Self nor non-Self, neither Being nor non-Being, neither consciousness nor non-consciousness. Universe, creation, Self, Being, presence, etc., are all features of consciousness. It is beyond all this, beyond all description. It is pure nothingness.

But this nothing is not an absence; it is Totality. In a way, we can say Brahman has a meta-existence, but it is not the being we knew prior. And it is equally true it is without that quality because it is without any quality.

Because we have transcended the covering value of consciousness but are very used to living within the dynamics of consciousness, Brahman is a big shift. It is without experience. Even the process of experience collapses when we step beyond consciousness. Describing this stage is thus quite paradoxical.

For example, this stage is sometimes called "Brahman Consciousness," but this is somewhat of an oxymoron due to Brahman being beyond or prior to consciousness. Where before it was consciousness knowing itself, now it is Brahman that is the knower of Brahman. We could say Brahman is conscious of itself. But it is not the flowing consciousness of Atman as it was in Unity. It is simply alert to its own nature.

As the highest kosha was Atman, we are now beyond the koshas as well.

We can also say Brahman is remembered. The knowing of itself returns. Unlike the stages of Unity, this does not involve the intellect. The knowing is more subtle but comprehensive.

Keep in mind that English words do not well describe this level of abstraction. Words like cause or structure, as they're normally used, are incorrect. We might think of the words here in their meta- or para- sense. They are used to point to the reality rather than describe it directly.

From this perspective, the world is not an illusion; it has never even come into existence. Something made from nothing will always be nothing. But the word "nothing" does not describe the profundity of Totality. It is not an emptiness, just a no-thingness. It is self-evident to itself alone. Brahman is the knower of Brahman.

> *Like the Absolute IS, Brahman is NOT.*
> *Brahman is not the Absolute.*
> *Brahman is not the relative.*
> *Brahman is not both of them together.*
> *Brahman is not neither [sic] of them.*
> *Brahman is The Knower.*
> — Maharishi Mahesh Yogi

Brahman is also known as the devourer; everything progressively becomes recognized as nothing but That.

> *...A hundred times this joy is the joy of the world of the ancestors...*
> *A hundred times the joy of the ancestors is the joy of the world of the Ghandarvans [music gods]...*
> *A hundred times the joy of the Ghandarvans is the joy of the world of the Devas [gods]...*
> *A hundred times the joy of the Devas is the joy of the world of Prajapati [the Creator]...*
> *A hundred times the joy of Prajapati is the joy of Brahman...*
>
> *This is the joy of one who is pure and free of desire. This is the supreme joy, the highest bliss, the world of the spirit.*
> — the sage Yagyavalkya[1]

This shift can happen prior to the unfoldment of much refined perception, but the perspective on what is transpiring is then completely different and may be quite a bit more muted.

One of the key markers of this shift is the falling away of the profound intimacy with all things found in Unity. That becomes the greatest barrier to this shift as we have to be willing to let it all go: the entire enlightenment, our relationship with God, and our intimacy with the world. Not everyone makes this shift. However, nothing is really lost in this shift, and Divinity soon arises in a far more profound way.

The distinction between uniting or retaining a relationship with the divine (discussed in the prior section) can be a major factor in how this process is experienced subjectively.

Two Steps

From the examples I'm aware of, it's common for this shift to come in two steps subjectively. The first is the falling away of the intimacy of Unity into something new that is neither fullness nor emptiness. We transcend Atman into an unknown. Brahman is not yet clear. In a small sampling, this took place with impersonal God Realization, merging with the divine. I have not discussed it with anyone who chose the personal form of God Realization yet. But if there has not been a Refined Unity stage, this shift would not be preceded by God Realization.

One friend found this stage "devastating" for a short while. Myself, I found it flat in a way I'd not experienced for some time. The richness had been sucked dry. This is not to suggest that this transition is a bad thing, only that it's not uncommon for there to be an initial falling away before what is now here is known.

This has been called the Shiva step where the old is destroyed.

In certain ways, the Brahman shift is similar to the initial waking of Self Realization. For some, there can be a falling away of the ego sense before the cosmic Self is recognized. Only now it is the cosmic Self that is falling away.

Similarly, just as the mind may try to regain control after awakening, the dynamics of consciousness may take time to wind down here. So there may be a bit of back and forth.

In the second step, we move more deeply into it and a new intensity unfolds and Brahman becomes clear or progressively clearer. Brahman begins to know Brahman.

In another case, a friend stepped through the door into Brahman, then back again a couple of times. When she made the final shift, she kept a great deal of the refined values. She thus had little of the first step.

This has been called the Shakti or Divine Mother step where she is the guru of Shiva and Shiva is the knower.

Brahman is also described as remembered, as we already are it.

The Experience

Now we have the paradoxical experience of the world appearing to the senses and yet we know directly that the world has never been created. Before we saw the divine or consciousness creating the world; now there is no such dynamic. There is just an appearance. The world doesn't exist AND yet there it is. (again, this is very different from world-as-illusion)

At first this can be a very curious experience, but soon it becomes normal. Then the paradox is only in trying to describe it.

This is illustrated by the sage Shankara:
> *Brahman is real*
> *the world is not real [the half truth]*
> *Brahman is the world*
> — Brahma Sutra Bhasya (Shankara's commentary)

> *The whole world is nothing but Brahman, the supreme.*
> — Mundaka Upanishad 2.2.12

The world appears to us because it is Brahman, not because it has reality in itself. It is as if Brahman has a brief musing and the result is the vastness of space and time and universes and beings.

> *It can never be that what is actually perceived is non-existent.*
> — Brahma Sutra Bhashya 2.2.28

Adyashanti has recently begun referring to this as his "no-Self" stage. It is the no-Self of post-Atman, post-consciousness. Bernadette Roberts has used the term in a similar way. This is distinct from the earlier "no-self" as the egolessness of Self Realization. This is a good example of how we need to understand how a term is being used to recognize what is being referred to.

Jerry Freeman makes a useful observation[2] about Brahman and ignorance. To paraphrase, Brahman requires Lesha Avidya (the faint remains of ignorance). There has to be enough of the sense of a person remaining for Brahman to be lived as a person. There is no Brahman without a knower of Brahman. Brahman is a human being in Brahman stage. Amusingly, ignorance is thus what makes the Great Awakening possible.

> *It is the non-Self that leads to Brahman Consciousness.*
> — Maharishi Mahesh Yogi[3]

Another distinction is that while consciousness is all about Self knowing itself, Brahman doesn't have that driver. The knowing is more subtle and self-evident.

As noted near the beginning, by this time Shiva-Shakti has descended to the root. The cosmic has come right to the level of the local body and then flows out into the world.

> *The world reveals Brahman.*
> — Maharishi Mahesh Yogi[4]

> *Atman is transcendental but Brahman is inclusive...*
> — Maharishi Mahesh Yogi[5]

As with other shifts, it is common for the Brahman shift to trigger another wave of unpacking. By this time, we're hopefully winding down what remains to be worked out. Life may now be dominated by the deeper flows of the cosmic. It has become less and less about residual habits of a person and more and more about the needs of the whole. But we remain human, however vast and inclusive awareness is. If we're in a body, there is still some karma at play. (There are rare beings who retain a physical body post-karma but that's another topic.)

Brahman comes to be inclusive of all prior stages simultaneously. Prior to Brahman, each stage is distinct and we leave behind the prior stage with each new stage. Now they are all available to us. Brahman stage is thus greater than all of them combined.

Because it is beyond even the subtle dualities of conscious or not, existing or not, Brahman resolves all paradoxes. It is true non-duality. But because it is a totality greater than all those dualities, it is inclusive of both. This makes it very difficult to describe.

The net result is that truth is now entirely dependent on what perspective you're looking from.

Uniqueness

Because the Brahman stage is the culmination of all the variations in the development of consciousness, it is lived right in the physiology and through the unique combination of the laws of nature that are here. Thus each person has a unique experience and expression of Brahman.

Summary

Brahman is the Great Awakening from Unity into Totality, beyond any prior conception of reality. It can be a bigger shift than any of the prior shifts and thus take longer to integrate and unfold. It's no longer the "experience and become" of Unity.

With Brahman established, the stages of consciousness are complete. Consciousness is fully awake to its own nature and origins. The process is now primarily the feminine: more and more refinement, Shakti bringing further abilities on-line, and so forth.

Example Descriptions

After being clearly awake in the oneness of Unity Consciousness, being everything everywhere for over 10 years and thinking there could not possibly be anything more, another completely unexpected and unbelievable shift happened.

Everything disappeared!! The sense of the existence of the body, world and universe and the Absolute Being/ Self disappeared (and has never returned). Everything remained the same, only the undeniable direct experience is that there is nothing here, and never has been. It is being prior to the sense of Being, the sense of existing, yet it includes the total range of all states of Consciousness. It is impossible to comprehend, even for someone in refined Unity Consciousness. It is the permanent state of being prior to Consciousness awake to itself. It is sublime.
— anonymous[6]

I suddenly became aware that nothing existed, nothing in the room or beyond, not even "me"!

In the room my voice spoke out loud "Oh my God, Oh my God" with open mouth and wide eyes in absolute awe/reverence/stunned wonder... no words can possibly explain the realization of that moment, suffice to

123

say there was a jaw dropping, immobilizing, transfixed stillness and disappearance beyond into Nothing!

It was as if "I" was now beyond anything, there was an appearance of the room and people but the "I" was "Source" and it was beyond Everything. In this place there was something so exquisite – joy, bliss and deep, deep abiding peace. The next short while, I was enraptured and could not find a voice. I just sat watching the appearance of the room and people in radiant bliss....

There was a knowing that I was prior to existence, pure, divine simplicity. I was beyond the illusion of Life as it had been. I was Life. It was as if I fell off the stage set of Life and realized that what "I" is, creates and contains all of what appears as Life. The nothing that I now was, was animating the mind body in the world and was creating the world of appearance.
— anonymous[7]

For the author, a merging with the Divine, my personal form of God, initiated the process. The merging ended the relationship, and it quickly became apparent that the intimacy with the world was gone too. At first I thought this unusual flatness was some brief period that would quickly pass. But it didn't. At the time, I was in grad school in classes six days a week so there was little time to just sit with it. Transcending Atman was not part of the understanding, and it took awhile to digest what had unfolded. When there was time to process it more, it deepened and what was here became clearer. This shift has been slower than the prior stages here. It is the vastest one yet.

It is useful to be reminded of the old saying: "If it can

be named, it is not the Tao." Few of these descriptions will make sense even for someone in advanced Unity. The purpose of this is to illustrate our potential and leave signposts for those traveling this way.

There can be the same greater or lesser clarity and the same greater or lesser refinement as before.

The Next Transition

Again, the refinement developed prior comes back in this new context. However, because of the degree of this shift beyond consciousness, there may be a larger pause before what had unfolded can be known in this new, vastly different context.

Notes

1 From The Yog Vasishtha and Taittiriya Upanishad 2:8

2 batgap.com/jerry-freeman/

3 *The Role of the Brahma Sutra in unfolding BC*, LaAntilla, January 23, 1973

4 *The Role of the Brahma Sutra in unfolding BC*, LaAntilla, January 23, 1973

5talk, Oct. 1993

6 L.W.: lucialorn.net/#!beyond-consciousness/cw8x

7 C.B.: lucialorn.net/#!beyond-consciousness/cw8x

Stage 3a
Refined Brahman

Far, far away the indweller of the house,
the Self, is seen reverberating.
— Rig Veda, 7.1.1

In the period through Self Realization and Unity, the refinement was through perception, the heart, and clarity of consciousness. Brahman is much more subtle than consciousness so the mechanism of consciousness now becomes an impediment.

Like a movie screen acts as a curtain for what is behind it, so too does the screen of consciousness impede the unfolding subtlety of knowing the holiness of Brahman.

It is impossible to understand or describe. Don't waste your time trying to figure it out or make a concept out of it. It can only be known by being it.
— Lorne Hoff[1]

Of course, Brahman itself doesn't refine. It is our ability to know it that does. In the sense that sattva increases bodily, the guna continues to play a role. But as Brahman is beyond the gunas, the deeper part of the process shifts into purity of Divinity rather than sattva.

This stage will happen in one of two ways:

1) If the covering quality of consciousness has been dissolving and there has been a God Consciousness or Refined Unity phase, the experience of Brahman will be flavoured this way and will naturally shift into Refined Brahman.

2) If consciousness is still dominant and little refined perception has occurred OR the stages in consciousness have unfolded rapidly, then the feminine side of the equation may have had little influence yet. Development may have been mostly internal and in consciousness alone. The person may spend much more time in Brahman and not progress here yet. More nothing, less divine.

I've seen people go through a God Consciousness process after Brahman, so this unfolds whenever it will.

If the first unfolds, once again we have a new perspective of the same refinement from prior stages.

I'll quote Lorne Hoff[2] on this:
> ... because it is prior to Consciousness itself, there is no perceiver, no perceiving and no perception. It is perpetually swelling in all the same divine flavors and qualities of wholeness and love as experienced previously, only in a finer more exquisite delicacy and fullness prior to

any possible distinction. It is nothingness, yet it is pure Divine power... This fullness of nothingness remains completely full yet uncaused.

In other words, "Refined Brahman" isn't about refinement of perception. It's about refining knowing: Brahman is the knower of Brahman.

What does it mean to say refined nothing? For this we can refer to a point Maharishi Mahesh Yogi discussed[3]:

Nirguna Brahm is Totality without qualities and unmanifest.
Saguna Brahm is Totality that is "becoming."

Maharishi described the mechanism of becoming as memory (Smriti). That remembers itself, stirring it into apparent qualities. But nothing more than this takes place.

The Source of Consciousness

In Brahman we discover the origin of consciousness. We can say there are two aspects or meta-qualities: alertness and liveliness. Alertness is what allows Brahman to know itself. Liveliness is what motivates that.

Liveliness stirs alertness to become aware. More liveliness and alertness flows, curves back on itself, and becomes self-aware. This is the origin of the dynamics of consciousness and its three-fold nature described near the beginning of the book: observer, process of observation, and observed. But from a Brahman perspective, this simply supports an appearance. It doesn't arise as something distinct or actually create something.

The creative intelligence within consciousness leads to the appearance of creation. It is as if consciousness takes a divine idea and makes a story of it we experience as creation. It is all just an idea or memory, uncaused. Nothing has ever happened. And yes that's a pun; Nothing Happens.

> *It is the subtle intention within nothingness to know itself.*
> — Lorne Hoff

The richness of this phase is a new profundity, intimacy, and oneness greater than everything prior. It is known directly, without any intermediary.

While Self has woken up to itself here prior, there are still vast swaths of creation that are not self-awake. From a Brahman perspective, the unawake is the non-Self. Brahman knows what is non-Self, the dark side that is silence alone, unlit by self-knowing, the light of awareness.

In the process of Brahman knowing itself it is said to devour the non-Self. When this happens in a person, they know it as awakening. Later, we discover the Divine impetus of this.

The Cosmic: Part 2

In The Cosmic section of Refined Unity, I introduced how we become (recognize ourselves as) cosmic, even on the level of the apparent individual body. We are the one body that is all bodies in all universes. With Brahman and the greater embodiment in form, we become cosmic physically. That is to say, our body is seen as cosmic even as it moves through its apparent day.

If this seems hard to grasp, consider your body-mind now. Even as an "individual," your body is composed of trillions of cells, each a complete life-form. They work as a coordinated whole to function as a body. The Cosmic is simply another natural scale of this, each person playing the role of a "cell" of the cosmic.

> *You Are Not an Individual; You Are a Republic*
> — Dr. R. Keith Wallace[4], physiologist

While I've discussed this with only a small number of people, what I've observed is that laws are enlivened or awoken and come on-line in the cosmic physiology. Quickly or over time, they integrate with existing active laws creating a new synthesis. This becomes the theme of this expression of the cosmic we refer to as a person.

For example, the synthesis of laws may express through an apparent person as bringing peace, catalyzing awakening, healing, or another style. We may observe said person making overt actions in the world or they may just go about their life while the action takes place on more subtle levels. Many of the very awake I know live fairly quiet lives.

In other words, this does not describe what an individual is doing but rather what is arising cosmically while the apparent person is going about life. Because the process is taking place cosmically, it includes vastly more than physical appearances. The interface for the cosmic to express is the devata body mentioned prior, but that is beyond the scope of this book to go into.

We could call the resulting expression the flavour of the darshan or presence. We also might relate to this as an advanced form of what Joan Harrigan spoke of as the post-descent rise to the energy center that will help embody this expression. The form this takes will vary widely. For many, their lives will go on more or less the same.

We could call this the process of embodiment. We come to live reality right on the surface, right in the (non-separate) relative world. Even the body is found to be limitless. And the nervous system comes to be composed of the finest relative values.

As this matures, we can say there is a sense of liberation of the person. The local expression loses constraints and can become a much fuller, richer expression of the local laws of nature. Eventually, even the physical body itself becomes a fluid body of light. That however is beyond the scope of what I know or have examples of.

Another aspect of the shift to the Cosmic is what is usually a gradual shift from purifying this body-mind to purifying progressively more cosmically. We shift from cleaning up our baggage to working on the entire load of humanity. In other words, there isn't an end to the clean-up job. But this isn't a bad thing. As you shift to a more cosmic perspective, it all becomes an aspect of who you are.

Those who have spent time in large groups doing spiritual practice together may have some sense of this. It can feel like you're processing other people's baggage in a kind of large washing machine, clearing the environment. This doesn't mean we take on others' stress. It means we purify the shared body-mind and heal the source of that behavior, just as we did prior more locally. We're healing the roots.

Clearing and healing on a more universal level is vastly more effective than personally. The more you clean, the clearer it all gets. And the cosmic is nothing new. It's simply the collected debris of apparent individuals who have always actually been cosmic.

> *When "I walk around" cosmic being moves attention through its musings, continuously purifying what is being experienced on all levels of creation. But nothing happens. And yet, this form talks and behaves in the world relatively normally because that takes care of itself. But nothing happens.*
> — author[5]

Cognition: Part 2

In the Refined Unity section, I outlined two stages of cognition. This third stage would not arise until after the Brahman stage is established.

3) Vedic or Primary Cognition

A Vedic cognition occurs when one "inscribes consciousness" with new knowledge, creating new principles or laws in creation. Those principles are now alive and intertwine with existing laws, creating new synergies and advancing the evolution of creation. This is the initial cognition of the Vedas themselves, adding to cosmic or divine memory or Smriti.

But here we have two ways of looking at it.

On the one hand, we have those key seers who had the primary cognitions described in the core Vedas. These cognitions structure the process of unfolding creation. They are said to inscribe smriti with their profound experience, adding to the memory or blueprints for our creation. Those memories can then be revived in later cycles of time with the prior styles of cognition.

With new laws of nature in creation, it progresses forward in its growth and evolution.

However, from a higher perspective, prior to creation there is no time so how can there be a first creation in which those cognitions inscribed memory? From this perspective, all of the cognitions are created together in a brief musing by the Divine. They form the blueprint of our creation. Within the cycles of creation, specific seers will arise in the allotted time and have those cognitions that unfold the next stage of creation.

Even more deeply, the inscriptions are reflections of the profound network of Shaktis in pure Divinity. (described in the next stage)

The effect of this is the same as the first. The difference is in origins: did the seer inscribe the memory or did the divine? Is there a fundamental difference at this point or only one in perspective?

The Vedas are the "sound not heard" existing as memory prior to experience. They are encoded with the seer destined to awaken the law of nature involved. I've also heard it described that the devata or law cognizes itself through the seer and the seer becomes the devata in the process. Each embodies the other.

Read any good translation of the core Vedas and you'll see them listed at the start of their cognition: rishi (seer), devata (law of nature), and chhandas (the metre or way the sound or vibratory values will express as creation). This starts the process in our universe. Rishi, devata, and chhandas are again another way to describe the observer, process, and object dynamics of consciousness mentioned prior.

As our body is actually cosmic and composed of devata, all the rishis are in our body.

Again, not everyone will have cognitions, but there is a very rich range of experience available to everyone who develops refined perception.

Summary

The process of Refined Unity continues, but now in this new context of Brahman. It varies widely how quickly Brahman settles in and thus how quickly the refined emphasis will take to unfold.

Example Descriptions

Daily life is quite ordinary in the most exquisite and extraordinary way! Each moment I move towards what motivates and inspires. Each moment is a surprise. To be a little less abstract – the mind still thinks and the body-mind experiences emotion and holds memory of the life of the person in certain preferences. There is pleasure in the most simple things, a transparency and ease to everything. There is no desire for any experience as everything is here right now. There is much spontaneous joy and laughter and also some raw emotional release which is sometimes accompanied with a narrative. I tend to prefer quiet and one to one connection over groups. There is comfort in the unknown and no need to know or plan anything.

Ultimately there is absolute freedom, God knowing, peaceful simplicity and Joy.
— anonymous[6]

For the author, what was present became progressively richer and fuller, with an intensity of light. The source of consciousness was revealed, along with the cosmic and the nature of cognition described above.

Notes

1 Describing this stage on his web site: lucialorn.net/states-of-consciousness

2 lucialorn.net/states-of-consciousness

3 Nov 2007: globalgoodnews.com/education-news-a.html?art=11961847844563398

4 Talk title, 2016

5 davidya.ca/2014/10/03/the-experience-follow-up/

6 CB: lucialorn.net/#!bc-shift2/cm21

Stage 3b
ParaBrahman

Pure holiness is found even in non-self nothingness.
— Lorne Hoff[1]

Para means beyond, or prior to, or supreme. It does not mean prior to nothing but rather greater even than Brahman. It is a progression of refinement and another range in this process.

As Brahman unfolds knowing, there comes a recognition of a deeper value that can only be described as Pure Divinity. However, Brahman itself cannot know pure Divinity. There has to be a shift towards pure Divinity for it to look upon itself.

For this to happen, Divinity is experienced as rising up into the physiology. This can be accompanied by new forms of clearing anything that impedes the process. Then we progressively become able to support it as a living reality. When this shift happens, it can dramatically amp up the presence and alertness, overshadowing the usual states of consciousness. It may disrupt sleep for a few days, somewhat like witnessing deep sleep might with the beginning of clear witnessing. Only here the alertness is exponentially greater.

As this first stage is integrated, it becomes recognized that everything has only ever been "pure Supreme Divinity in appearance." (Lorne Hoff) It is the ultimate cause; it is pure grace. All prior sense of origin including being, consciousness, creative intelligence, and all of creation is recognized as an appearance of pure Divinity. Everything we have experienced has only ever been pure Divinity.

We could say it is an even higher recognition of divine holiness, beyond all that was surrendered in the transition into Brahman. It is not an expressed divinity that may have been known prior but pure Divinity itself.

Once the first stage of rising into the physiology is sufficiently established, a second stage begins. Now, a higher value of Divinity descends, much like the descent of consciousness through the higher stages. In fact, it begins much like another awakening and we can feel quite abstracted from our prior sense of being. Only now it is Divinity awakening to its own detail.

This takes over the prior sense of observing consciousness. We experience pure Divinity as looking out through the senses. In other words, it completes the process of moving out of stages in consciousness.

What is Pure Divinity?

In the prior refined sections, we spoke of the divine in form or formless. But this was qualified divinity, divinity in some value of expression. It is some aspect of divinity being embodied. So what is Pure Divinity, beyond all qualifications?

This is far beyond belief. Even the mechanism of experience in consciousness has been transcended. Yet it is still something we can live.

We can say Divinity is Omnipresent, it is everything. But it is not the appearance of the world alone. It is what is behind that, the profound intelligence and energy that supports the world appearance.

Omniscient is also used to describe Divinity. It is profoundly self-knowing, supporting all the flow of energy and laws of nature that sustain the careful balance of the world.

Divinity is said to be Omnipotent. All the energy in the universe is a tiny reflection of the potency of Divinity. It is the ultimate causality, the first and final cause.

Love in its pure form is the flow of Divinity.

Divinity is fundamental to our very being. We are in and of the Divine. Our very awareness and the sense that I Am are qualities of Divinity.

Divinity is completely self-sufficient and requires no creation or tapestry of consciousness. The Divine is known without a knower as it is a totality of all-knowing alertness. It is an ocean of light. But this is not the light of perception and objects. It is simply self-illumined.

As may be apparent, those fundamental meta-qualities we recognized prior – alertness and liveliness – are now known to be qualities of the Divine. They allowed Brahman to know itself and led to the dynamics of consciousness and all of apparent creation.

The essence of pure Divinity is a totality far greater than any conception, even if a conception is used for the purposes of devotion. How else can we relate to such immense totality?

In a curious way, we could say the divine is fully networked. The pure power of Divinity knowing the totality of itself creates internal Shaktis, intentions of pure power. This causes uncreated threads of connection that allow the brief musing of Divinity to be fully known from a vast array of perspectives simultaneously without creating anything.

As a side effect, alertness becomes simple self-awareness, leading to the self-interacting dynamics of consciousness. This sets the stage for consciousness to weave a tapestry of these threads, to unfold the divine musing as if in a stage play, a Lila. This creates the appearance of creation where there is nothing but pure Divinity, uncreated, yet appearing and seeming to unfold.

Because of the mechanism we're using to know Divinity, it may unfold in seven steps, beginning from the bottom of the chart below. For example, knowing the shaktis or threads described above would be the second step.

The Structure of Divinity

	Quality	In Creation	In the World
7	Divine Alertness	Primary Divinity	
6	Divine Liveliness	recognition, consciousness	
5	Divine Intention	causality	space
4	Divine Love	flow, love	air
3	Divine Power	power, mind	fire
2	Divine Action	shakti, energy	water
1	Divine Being	presence	earth

If we think of the chakras or koshas or cosmic body as a reflection of "as above, so below," it may give some sense of these stages of unfolding within divinity.

Pure Divinity itself has no "layers" or stages. And yet, Divinity is what produced those layers by which it would be known. Once embodied, the stage is set to know Divinity itself.

At this point, I have not seen a text discussing this and have insufficient examples to corroborate it. I expect the model to refine.

As pure Divinity becomes known, we recognize places where She has shown up in life events. Her pure white light shows up at birth, grace, the drop at makara, awakening, forms of the divine, death... and the call home.

The Cosmic: Part 3

The expression of the nervous system [is] structured in the unexpressed value of the Absolute
— Maharishi Mahesh Yogi[2]

In ParaBrahman, the Cosmic is also recognized not as consciousness but as pure Divinity. Even the physical body is recognized as threads of divinity, profound self-knowing. Physical, cosmic, and Divine all merge.

In a Q&A on development post-Brahman, Maharishi Mahesh Yogi said:

Earthly nervous system could evolve to as many levels as we can mention and ultimately to a conceivable level of supreme relative matter (celestial)...it will be still localized, because it is relative. Only the quality of relativity will be supreme...

And then if our imagination could permit us to conceive of a nervous system or a structure of the Absolute – we can intellectually conceive of a structure of the Absolute. This then will be non-localized.
— Maharishi Mahesh Yogi[3]

One way we might understand this is that our nervous, circulatory, and lymphatic systems are founded on an energy system of nadis or energy tubes that guide prana or life energy. (see The Chakras section) The nadis are formed by flowing consciousness curving back on itself, spiraling into tubes. And in turn, those tubes follow the threads of Shakti.

As our physiology is purified and untangled from our physicality, we progressively recognize and then embody subtler and subtler values of reality, eventually resulting in the structure of the absolute Maharishi described. It becomes clear why progressive clarity dominates after the stages in consciousness have unfolded.

Cognition: Part 3

From the perspective of pure Divinity, the "inscribing" of consciousness by Vedic cognition is the awakening of a Shakti (thread of Divinity) to express in creation, joining the tapestry, as it were. These are the literal sutras that awaken laws of nature described prior. We might call this the structure of Divinity. Their awakening becomes the memory or blueprint of creation.

Summary

The refinement and progressive embodiment of Divinity and fluidity continues. In the current time, our full potential is unknown. In higher ages with longer lives, the refinement of the physiology and unfolding took place over hundreds of years in a more supportive atmosphere. Given our current constraints, we do what we can.

Some rare beings have developed sattva to such a degree it becomes physically visible. They are effulgent, glowing with golden light. As this is strongest in the head, it's most noticeable there, hence the halos in Christian, Hindu, and other iconography.

Many lifetimes ago, I went on a pilgrimage to see such a person in what is now the South-West United States. He was so bright, he was hard to look at. I've seen a historical reference to him as well as a few others.

However, this is also a prescribed siddhi (ability) in the Yog Sutra. Thus a person may gain or culture the ability. It is not "sign" in and of itself.

I mention this mainly because I anticipate examples arising i the near future.

There are various other traditions, myths, and rumours abou the consequences of these unfolding stages. It's best to be ser sible about these ideas. A common one, for example, is tha enlightenment means we're done with human lifetimes. Bu this rather depends on how mature the process is when w die. If we have not wound down our entanglements, they wi call us back to another lifetime, however clear the shifts.

In other words, it's not just about awakening but establishin a mature embodiment.

Notes
1 Said during retreat, January 18, 2014
2 *Brahman Consciousness – Pure Absolute Being Lived By The Body Of T Absolute*, Hertenstein, 1974
3 Hertenstein, 1974

Embodiment

Embodiment is not something that you do; it is some-thing that is a result of how far you take enlightenment and how much of yourself you give to it. The entire cos-mos is your body. Let your humanness reflect and mani-fest the whole.
— Adyashanti, *The Impact of Awakening*

This book describes the opening shifts and the integra-tion process that follows. But this is just the ground on which day-to-day life will be lived. The stages are not an end in themselves but rather the platform for living a fuller, richer life well beyond any description.

There are quite a few influences that will determine the way these stages will express through this or that per-son. There isn't a one-size-fits-all appearance or style we should expect of someone enlightened. Rather, ev-ery process and embodiment is unique. Here are some of the major variables.

Householder or Renunciate Orientation

Most people are born householders. It's how they're wired and is necessary for the continuation of the species. They'll be living in the world through experiences and relationships. A renunciate on the other hand will emphasize transcendence and non-identity.

We're not long out of a dark age where spiritual progress commonly required spending substantial time withdrawing from the mud of the world, even for householders. That time is over but there is still a strong momentum in spiritual and religious teachings that emphasize a monastic approach. When someone follows a path they're unsuited to, they're obliged to act in unnatural ways. Strain and problems arise. Celibacy, for example, is not natural for most people. Moderation is the better guide.

This is also not about appearances or going through the motions. Some may adopt a monk's role for a time but it may not serve them well long-term. On the other hand, this distinction may not be obvious from surface appearances. For example, I know someone who's married and owns a home but lives a renunciate lifestyle dominated by spiritual practice. There's no avoidance there, just a natural inclination.

Emphasizing Atman or Emphasizing Sattva

Some people are naturally more consciousness-focused (atman) and some will be more focused on feeling, healing, energy awareness, and so forth (sattva). This emphasis is determined mainly by our dominant laws of nature. Unlike Orientation, this emphasis is on a spectrum. Some people are very transcendental and some just a bit, some are very energy-centered, some just a bit.

While a consciousness focus is common for renunciates, they're not equivalent. Men in general can be inclined this way also, but it's certainly not universal. Similarly, you'll see more women in healing and energy groups but some men also.

Further, our practices will tend to amplify one side or the other. A long practice of deep meditation will amplify our sense of consciousness. Work with energy awareness and healing will amplify that side. But we'll also tend to favour practices that are related to our approach, so we're more likely to amplify our existing emphasis.

This is an arena where balance is useful. If we're more transcendent, it's good to bring balance with heart culturing. Conversely, someone heart-centered may need grounding in pure being, in source beyond energy. Nothing forced or unnatural to the person, just some balancing.

Temperament

People tend to be introverted or extroverted. This is another spectrum of degree. While a renunciate may be inclined to be introverted, that's not necessarily the case and introversion doesn't mean renunciate. Both orientations can be either.

Dominant Path: Intellect, Heart, and Body

Our Path is another inclination driven by our dominant laws of nature. We'll naturally be more heart-
oriented, more mind-oriented, or relate more with the
body, perception, and doing.

You see this in the Yoga traditions of India: Bhakti Yoga
(devotion) for the heart, Gyani Yoga (intellect) for the
conceptual, Karma Yoga (action) for action and perception, and Hatha Yoga for the body itself.

There is a broad tendency to relate a conceptual approach to the masculine side, consciousness, and renunciates. Similarly, one who is energy-focused will
also tend to be more heart-focused. You see a lot more
women in those groups.

But we shouldn't confuse one to mean the other as we
are each complex blends of laws of nature. Individual
blends of the above will show up in all sorts of varieties.

It's also an incorrect understanding to think we're just
a Bhakti or Gyani or whichever. Most of us are blends
with an emphasis that shifts over time.

Our stage of development will also tend to amplify different approaches. For example, the approach and shift
of awakening will often shift our relationship to action.
The awakening heart of God Consciousness will amplify devotional tendencies even in non-devotees. And
Unity calls for the discrimination of the fine intellect
even in the heart-oriented.

The sage Shankara revived the monastic tradition in India and had four primary disciples. Three of them were gyanis (intellects) but Trotaka was a devotee, on a heart path. As it worked out, he was the first to become enlightened. He was a renunciate devotee with a strongly consciousness-based emphasis.

I'm a householder but have a strong consciousness-based and conceptual approach naturally. The masculine approach is prominent but there's lots of subtle perception. Yet while I'm quite conceptual, my dominant Yoga is Karma, the path of action and perception, of experiences. The concepts are driven by experiences rather than the intellect.

A friend of mine is very much the householder running multiple businesses. While he has a significant devotional tendency, his prominent path is also through doing and experiencing. In fact, karma yogis are very common in the West.

You'll also see the intellectual energy healer, the body-oriented extrovert householder, and many nuanced variations.

It's also useful to note that a devotion to knowledge or right action is still a form of devotion. Discrimination of the intellect plays a part in right action and so forth. Again, the paths are not exclusive.

Dominant Sense

Another major filter that can affect how all the above is perceived is which sense we favour, our dominant sense. For example, I'm very visual and because I'm on a perceptual path, I often learn by seeing and being shown things. And I tend to use visual language. Others will be much more attuned to feeling and touch or sound. I discussed this prior in the God Consciousness section (1a).

While there can be correlations between Path and Dominant Sense, that's by no means universal.

Dominant Laws of Nature

Our DNA is mostly the same as everyone else's; it takes just a few variations to create our unique physiology. So, too, with our laws of nature. Amplify a few specific ones and you get our distinctive gifts and approach to life. I've mentioned some previously but there are many other possible distinctive qualities. Someone may naturally challenge others, for example. Or have an affinity for other languages.

I've also mentioned how we can embody new laws of nature in later stages of development.

Cycles of Time

There are also various influences of the cycles of time that will tend to shift our emphasis for a while. For example, a long illness or age may incline us to a more inner-directed life. But that doesn't make it our orientation, just a phase.

For some of us, our background didn't culture our natural inclinations. We may need some experiences and experiments to find our natural route. Please don't use a list like this to determine yours. This is not a conceptual exercise but one of finding what is smooth and natural for us through direct experience. Funnily enough, some of it may not be obvious to us because it's so natural and normal. We're born with it and take it for granted and have never developed an internal dialog about it. Often, we have to drop some expectations of what our life is supposed to look like to see what is actually here. Doesn't that sound like typical awakening advice?

Closing

We shall not cease from exploration,
and the end of all our exploring
will be to arrive where we started
and know the place for the first time.
— T.S. Elliot, from *Four Quartets*

This book was designed to offer a working framework for our natural potential, far beyond self-actualization.

While once I could count on one hand the number of people I'd heard of who were enlightened, now I've lost count – even of the people whose awakening I've witnessed. I've met many, many more living the spectrum described in this book. I've also seen that as more people live this, it becomes easier for others.

To put all of this in a larger perspective, I can point to the Kala (meaning time or attribute) model. This is an ancient 16-level evolutionary model, based on skills and abilities. Plants are a 1, water-born animals are a 2, egg-born a 3, and womb-born (mammals) a 4. Humans range from 4, on par with other mammals, up to about 7 or so. (5-9 sound similar to the post-personal stages but the translations are unclear) Buddha is said to be a 10, Rama a 12-14 and Krishna a 16 at the top of the scale. A fully enlightened human is thus about half of an avatar (form) of God.

On an avatar, Maharishi Mahesh Yogi[1] clarifies:

> *The unmanifested in form, not manifested in form. The Absolute has not become relative. The unmanifested has not become manifested. Remaining absolute, it has assumed a form.*

An avatar remains absolute even though in appearance. Humans, on the other hand, are working back toward that.

The mind may try to structure grand concepts out of this book but those can be a barrier to realization. Our concepts are never it because post-personal stages are beyond the mind.

> *Knowledge in books, remains in books.*
> — old Sanskrit proverb

Treat this as a work in progress or working model, not fixed ideas to believe. It is designed to be a map, not the journey itself. Don't fall into the trap of debating the true road – the path is found in realization. All paths lead to the same place, however we might describe them.

No matter where you go, there you are.
— Buckaroo Banzai[2]

Enjoy your natural potential.
Davidya

Notes

1 Kumbha Mela, 1966
2 From the movie *Buckaroo Banzai across the 8th Dimension*

Bibliography

Adyashanti. (2009). *The End of Your World: Uncensored Straight Talk on the Nature of Enlightenment.* Boulder, CO: Sounds True.

Adyashanti. (2011). *Falling into Grace: Insights on the End of Suffering.* Boulder, CO: Sounds True.

Alexander, Charles N., Langer, Ellen J. (Eds). (1990) *Higher Stages of Human Development: Perspectives on Adult Growth.* New York, NY: Oxford University Press. [out of print]

Campbell, Anthony. (1974). *Seven States of Consciousness: A Vision of Possibilities Suggested by the Teaching of Maharishi Mahesh Yogi.* New York, NY: Harper & Row. [out of print]

Caplan, Mariana. (1999). *Halfway Up the Mountain: The Error of Premature Claims to Enlightenment.* Prescott, AZ: Hohm Press.

Egenes, Thomas (trans.). (2010). *Maharishi Patanjali Yoga Sutra.* Fairfield, IA: 1st World Publishing.

Harrigan, Joan. (2005). *Kundalini Vidya: The Science of*

Spiritual Transformation (6th ed.). Knoxville, TN: Patanjali Kundalini Yoga Care (self-published).

Goldberg, Philip. (2010). *American Veda: From Emerson and the Beatles to Yoga and Meditation: How Indian Spirituality Changed the West.* New York, NY: Harmony Books.

Katz, Vernon. (2011, 2014). *Conversations with Maharishi: Maharishi Mahesh Yogi Speaks about the Full Development of Human Consciousness, Vol. 1 & 2.* Fairfield, IA: MUM Press.

Pearson, Craig. (2008). *The Complete Book of Yogic Flying.* Fairfield, IA: MUM Press.

Pearson, Craig. (2013). *The Supreme Awakening: Experiences of Enlightenment Throughout Time – and How You Can Cultivate Them.* Fairfield, IA: MUM Press.

Mahesh Yogi, Maharishi. (1967/1990). *On the Bhagavad-Gita: A New Translation and Commentary with Sanskrit Text, Chapters 1 to 6.* London, UK: Arkana: Penguin Books.

Mahesh Yogi, Maharishi. (1963/2001). *Science of Being and Art of Living: Transcendental Meditation.* New York, NY: Meridian: Plume: Penguin.

Travis, Frederick. (2012). *Your Brain is a River, Not a Rock.* Amazon Createspace.

Venkatesananda, Swami. (1993). *Vasishtha's Yoga.* Albany, NY: State University of New York.

Web References
for mentioned People & Organizations

Adyashanti: adyashanti.org
Aurobindo: sriaurobindoashram.org/ashram/sriauro/
Bernadette Roberts: bernadetteroberts.blogspot.ca
Bernardo Kastrup: bernardokastrup.com
Buddha at the Gas Pump: batgap.com
Byron Katie: byronkatie.com
David Chalmers: consc.net
Eckhart Tolle: eckharttolle.com
Fred Travis: drfredtravis.com
Gangaji: gangaji.org
Jerry Freeman: facebook.com/jerry.freeman.98499
Joan Harrigan: kundalinicare.com
Kristin Kirk: kristinkirk.com
Loch Kelly: lochkelly.org
Lorne & Lucia Hoff: lucialorn.net
Maharishi Mahesh Yogi:
tmhome.com/books-videos/maharishi-mahesh-yogi-tm
Mariana Caplan: realspirituality.com
Neelam: neelam.org
Patanjali Kundalini Yoga Care: kundalinicare.com
Peter Mayer: petermayer.com
Rose Rosetree: rose-rosetree.com
Susanne Cook-Greuter: cook-greuter.com
Susanne Marie: susannemarie.org
Transcendental Meditation: tm.org

Many of the books topics can be explored in other articles on the authors web site: davidya.ca

Index

Acknowledgments

Some of this book was originally part of a much larger text that was never published. There have been many, many influences in the decade since while my experience and understanding has grown and refined.

To Maharishi Mahesh Yogi for the techniques and the fundamental understanding he offered. Both have served me very well and created the foundation on which this unfolding and this book were built.

To Lorne & Lucia Hoff for creating the space that allowed what was here to flower and for support along the way.

To the many people who have had shifts while I was there or shared with me later. Their experience has heavily informed the understanding in this book and broken many preconceptions.

For the book itself, I wish to offer thanks:
To the numerous authors and publishers who have offered feedback and recommendations along the way.
To *ProWritingAid* software for helping polish the text prior to editing.
To Tim Owens for his editing wisdom and support.

About

The Author:
David Buckland began the spiritual journey in the mid-70's. His interest in consciousness and his meditation practice have continued for more than 40 years.

He began using the nickname "Davidya" as an online pen-name in 2007 soon after awakening. The name took on a life of it's own.

In 2011, he earned an MA in Vedic Science, studying Vedic literature, Sanskrit, and world religions.

See the Preface for the timeline of the spiritual unfolding. You can also visit: davidya.ca/about

The Book:
Further copies and other formats of this book can be ordered though the web site at:
davidya.ca/books

The Publisher:

Davidya Publishing
Courtenay, BC, Canada V9N 3W5
books@davidya.ca

27702021R00108

Printed in Great Britain
by Amazon